THE CHURCH THAT CARES

IDENTIFYING AND RESPONDING TO NEEDS IN YOUR COMMUNITY

KENNETH R. MILLER
MARY ELIZABETH WILSON

Illustrated by
Stacey Elliott

Judson Press® Valley Forge

Dedicated to those churches and church members
who have striven faithfully to develop caring
relationships between congregation and community.

THE CHURCH THAT CARES

Copyright © 1985
Judson Press, Valley Forge, PA 19482-0851

Bible quotations in this volume are from the Revised Standard Version of the Bible
copyrighted 1946, 1952 © 1971, 1973 by the Division of Christian Education of the
National Council of the Churches of Christ in the U.S.A., and used by permission.

Library of Congress Cataloging-in-Publication Data

Miller, Kenneth R.
   The church that cares.

   Bibliography: p.
   1. Church work. 2. Church and social problems— United States. 3. Church and
the world. 4. Pastoral theology. 5. United States—Social conditions— 1960-
I. Wilson, Mary Elizabeth. II. Title.
BV4406.U6M54 1985   259   85-14786
ISBN 0-8170-1087-4

The name JUDSON PRESS is registered as a trademark in the U.S. Patent Office.
Printed in the U.S.A.

Contents

Preface

Deeply caring love was the mark by which the early Christians were known in their communities. As Tertullian, an early church father, put it: "It is our care for the helpless, our practice of lovingkindness, that brands us in the eyes of our opponents. 'Only look,' they say, 'look how they love one another. . . . Look how they are prepared to die for one another.'"[1] Caring love was the bridge by which the early believers went out of the church into the world God so loved, and also the bridge that brought many from the community into the fellowship of Christ and the church.

The caring of people in the early church went beyond the word to the deed as they followed Christ's example in providing for the less fortunate—the widow, the orphan, the sick, the poor, the oppressed. There is a need today to recapture the wholeness of the gospel. In his tract entitled *Two Half-Gospels or a Whole?* William R. Herzog II puts the challenge this way:

> Now it appears that we are in a position to learn some valuable lessons from our recent history. If we can root ourselves in a vision of the gospel that is built neither on the half truth that gospel equals saving souls, nor on the other half truth that gospel equals saving society, we may be able to construct a full vision of preaching the whole Good News.[2]

The question is rhetorical, of course, because there is not a choice if we understand the gospel!

The closest frontier for the church's caring love today is in many of the communities of which our churches are a part. The presence of many immigrants is significantly changing the landscapes of our communities! This is true without even mentioning the earlier minorities who are still struggling to achieve acceptance, self-esteem, and self-reliance in our society. Then there are those persons of special need who because of endowment, misfortune, or handicap have not been able to participate in the full benefits of our society. It is in our nearby neighborhoods and communities

5

where need takes on a face and we see the person's pain that we can best fashion a caring response.

This book is written for local church leaders to help them become aware of community needs, identify the many resources of the church for caring, and fashion appropriate responses in community ministry.

The authors wish to express a particular word of thanks to several persons whose published works proved especially insightful and stimulating in the writing of this book. Those kind mentors are Dieter T. Hessel, Harry Fagan, Gregory F. Pierce, and Speed B. Leas. Their experience and knowledge of the Christian social action field not only makes us indebted as colleagues, but again reminds us that we experience the unity of Christ's church most truly when we are yoked in a common mission of justice and reconciliation in the world. Thank you, brothers in the faith.

Kenneth R. Miller
Mary Elizabeth Wilson

1

Jesus Calls Us to Caring

And one of them, a lawyer, asked him a question, to test him. "Teacher, which is the great commandment in the law?" And he said to him, "You shall love the Lord your God with all your heart, and with all your soul, and with all your mind. This is the great and first commandment. And a second is like it, You shall love your neighbor as yourself. On these two commandments depend all the law and the prophets" (Matthew 22:35-40).

$\mathbf{T}$he parable of the good Samaritan (Luke 10:25-37) was spoken in answer to a question posed by a religious teacher to test Jesus' faithfulness to the Jewish Law. When Jesus turned the question back on him, the teacher responded that the essence of the Law was love for God and neighbor, but in an attempt to justify himself he asked, "Who *is* my neighbor?"

Jesus Cared About the Whole Person

Jesus' telling of the story about the good Samaritan reveals a lot about how Jesus understood the gospel message. The parable deals with personal relationships of love toward God *and* neighbor. It calls us to care for the needs of the whole person—spiritual *and* physical. And it inseparably connects the two to make both essential parts of the gospel itself!

Jesus' teachings expressed concern for the whole person. Three of Jesus' parables (the lost sheep, the lost coin, and the lost son in Luke 15:1-32) underscore God's valuing of each and every individual, regardless of life situation, and they express God's joy in the restoration of lost persons to right relationships with their Creator and Redeemer.

In the Sermon on the Mount (Matthew 5–7) Jesus indicates that God is a heavenly parent who appreciates the unique character and needs of human creations—sons and daughters of God. God's children are to trust God not only for God's grace and love but also for the most basic of human physical needs—food, drink, and clothing. Jesus also lifted up the legitimacy of such concerns in the Lord's Prayer (perhaps more appropriately "The Disciples' Prayer") when he said, "Give us this day our daily bread" (Matthew 6:11).

When speaking of the final judgment in Matthew 25, Jesus made a clear connection between true discipleship and compassion for persons with basic needs:

"Then the righteous will answer him, 'Lord, when did we see thee hungry and feed thee, or thirsty and give thee drink? And when did we see thee a stranger and welcome thee, or naked and clothe thee? And when did we see thee sick or in prison and visit thee?' And the King will answer them, 'Truly, I say to you, as you did it to one of the least of these my brethren, you did it to me'" (Matthew 25:37-40).

Jesus' care for whole persons was also expressed by his own actions. He not only offered his presence to the isolated and lonely man who had leprosy but also healed him of the dread disease (Matthew 8:1-4). He not only offered forgiveness of sins to the woman caught in adultery but also provided a healing acceptance that would help her restore constructive social relationships (John 8:1-11). He not only raised Lazarus from death but also personally identified with Mary and Martha in their deep grief and loneliness (John 11:1-44).

He not only taught the five thousand people about God and the kingdom but also fed them when they had grown faint from hunger (Luke 9:10-17).

Jesus Cared About Persons in Their Community Setting

Jesus' ministry led him to many of the towns and villages of Galilee and Judea. The persons he cared about were in community situations which could contribute both to their plight and to their deliverance.

Representative of such communities was Jerusalem, the seat of the Jewish nation. The Scriptures depict Jesus weeping over the city as he approached it for the final time (Luke 19:41-44). Perhaps he wept because all of the political, religious, and social issues that dramatically influenced the lives of the people converged in that community. He saw the contradictions of the city's promise and plight and lamented its unwillingness to become the just and humane society foreshadowed by the prophets.

Roman totalitarianism and militarism held the city in its tight, often ruthless grip. Raw, naked power was what Rome respected most. This was demonstrated some years ago in the movie entitled *Ben Hur*—particularly in the chariot-racing scene. Roman chariot drivers placed blades on their rotating wheel hubs that would destroy their competitors' wheels like a buzz saw! Rome had little but contempt for its well-to-do alien subjects, and it had no sympathy or compassion for the weak and powerless. Any accommodation with local Jewish leadership was prompted by its own political self-interest in keeping the peace. This was grossly illustrated in the travesty of Jesus' trial before Pontius Pilate and in the cruel punishment of crucifixion.

Religious traditionalism had encrusted the teachings of the Torah in hundreds of rabbinical legalisms. The cries of the Old Testament prophets for justice had fallen on deaf ears. An evidence of this erosion of truly human and spiritual values was seen in Jesus' healing of the man with the withered hand (Mark 3:1-6) and in the Pharisees' criticism that Jesus had violated the sabbath by this act of compassion!

Practical materialism and opportunism abounded with Rome's exploitation of the weak and callous disregard for the poor. The Roman oppressors exacted heavy revenues from their subjects to support their political and military dominance. Certain Jewish tax collectors had formed liaisons with their despised Roman occupiers for personal gain

which had resulted in their alienation from their own people. Jesus surprised his detractors by offering a relationship to one such tax collector named Zacchaeus (Luke 19:1-10). Jesus became his house guest and rescued him from loneliness and greed.

Jesus Cared for Persons by Confronting Community Justice Issues

Jesus' concern focused heavily on persons who were the "down-and-outers" of society. His announcement of his mission in the synagogue at Nazareth was couched in the prophetic language of Isaiah:

> "The Spirit of the Lord is upon me,
> because he has anointed me to preach good news to the poor.
> He has sent me to proclaim release to the captives
> and recovering of sight to the blind,
> to set at liberty those who are oppressed,
> to proclaim the acceptable year of the Lord"
> —Luke 4:18-19.

These words signaled his intention to be the champion of society's underdogs—those neglected by society because they were not useful, those rejected because they were not acceptable, those exploited because they were not powerful, and those oppressed because they were not tolerable. Jesus himself associated with the poor and social outcasts: "Why do you eat and drink with tax collectors and sinners?" (Luke 5:30). He disdained class and privilege (the Pharisees loved the "best seats in the synagogues and salutations in the market places" Luke 11:43). He broke through the barriers of racism and sexism (the Samaritan woman at the well, John 4:1-30), and he angrily confronted economic exploitation in the guise of religion (the money changers in the temple, Matthew 21:12-13).

In the course of championing the downtrodden, Jesus found it necessary to confront the community attitudes and issues that contributed to oppression of all kinds. In the case of the temple money changers and pigeon sellers, Jesus was protesting the economic exploitation of the poor who could not afford the more pretentious sacrifices for worship. He accused the merchandisers of making a "den of robbers" out of a "house of prayer."

Jesus broke two unjust social conventions when he encountered the woman at the well. First of all, as a man he *initiated* a conversation with a woman. Second, as a Jew he engaged in conversation with a Samaritan, a race despised by his countrymen. By his intentional nonconformity he opposed the major discriminations of his culture.

Militarism and violence were also issues that Jesus confronted. The Roman military establishment, which had conquered and subjugated Palestine, brought violent reaction from some of the Jews. The Zealots were a fanatical Judean group who were consistently opposed to and in rebellion against the Romans. There is a possibility that the disciple named Simon, who according to Luke 6:15 was called "the Zealot," may have been aligned with this group. At the time of Jesus' betrayal by Judas, one of Jesus' followers drew a sword in his defense. He was told by Jesus, "put your sword back into its place; for all who take the sword will perish by the sword" (Matthew 26:52). Jesus embraced a nonviolent approach to injustice as illustrated by his own self-giving death on the cross.

Community Justice Issues Affect People Today

Justice issues continue to affect our communities today. They may differ in feature and scope, but in many instances they resemble those that Jesus confronted in his day.

International differences and the resulting arms race threaten not only our national security but also the proportion of our resources available for human services and community programs. Growing immigrant and refugee populations in many areas of our country strain our community services and challenge our ability to accept, welcome, and assist persons of varying ethnic origins who are seeking refuge, freedom, and opportunity in our nation. The heightened aspirations of women for personal and vocational fulfillment are also impacting the social roles of men, children, the elderly, and families in our communities. The technological revolution has produced concern for how people in our neighborhoods will be equipped to earn their "daily bread," and it has raised questions about the limited supply, safe retrieval, environmental pollution, and fair application of our natural resources.

While these issues touch all of us in one way or another, they will particularly impact the minorities in our society who are struggling to achieve economic and social stability. Growing numbers of these persons are represented in our denominational families and increasingly in the neighborhoods and communities of which our churches are a part. It is in these nearby arenas that we have the greatest opportunity to experience the need and to help create a truly caring community. It is in these settings that the struggle for human dignity, self-esteem, self-reliance, and self-fulfillment can be seen in the faces of our "neighbors." Jesus' question in the parable of the good Samaritan was not "Who is my neighbor?" but "Whose neighbor am I?" The church as the body of Christ in the world must incarnate his love and care for those around us in the neighborhoods, villages, towns, and cities of today!

In the next chapter you will find help in taking a caring look at *your* community!

2

A Caring Look at Your Community

When he saw the crowds, he had compassion for them, because they were harassed and helpless, like sheep without a shepherd (Matthew 9:36).

At the age of twenty-five Walter Rauschenbusch became the pastor of the Second German Baptist Church which was located on the edge of Hell's Kitchen, one of New York City's notorious slums. As he ministered among the poor he saw firsthand how poverty, disease, overcrowding, and economic exploitation destroyed the souls of people. What he saw convinced him that social institutions as well as individual persons must be evangelized; and he began to read the Bible from this new perspective. In his book *Christianity and the Social Crisis* he wrote:

> The prophets were public men and their interest was in public affairs. Some of them were statesmen of the highest type. All of them interpreted past history, shaped present history, and foretold future history on the basis of the conviction that God rules with righteousness in the affairs of nations, and that only what is just, and not what is expedient and profitable, shall endure.[1]

Jesus' caring about persons and their communities led him to focus on people who were victims of social injustice. Many of these same justice issues are present in the communities your church is called to serve today. As you begin to discover your community, you will identify issues to which you can respond with caring. First get an overview (a general idea of who and what exists in the community) and determine power structures and patterns of influence. Later, narrow your concern to a specific goal. While your initial task is to discover the community, you will want to do that by focusing on a target area.

The church building itself frequently serves as a "physical" witness of God's presence in the community. By just being there, the church is already a testimony to newcomers and community members who pass by. The one-mile radius around the church is often considered its geographical community. In rural areas the town or the county may be considered the church's community. As you go out from your church you will want to discover who lives in, works in, or passes through this geographical area. Our neighbor is defined for us first by geography, but distances can be shortened by our mobility and our caring which makes us closer to others. Our community is a network of human relationships as well as a place.

Lines have to be drawn somewhere in order for your congregation to take initial responsibility for defining goals for ministry in the community. We will call this your "sphere of influence." In developing a community ministry goal, there may be some geographical overlapping of church location, member residences, and persons in need or issues calling for attention. As you determine your sphere of influence, keep your boundaries flexible.

Plunge into the Community

An initial activity for discovering needs and issues within your community will be to "plunge" into your community. We often take for granted the things that are most familiar to us. A creative way to discover your community is to lead church members out of the church building and into the

neighborhood—out of their cars and onto their feet, out of images of who and what's out there, and into experiences of the people and places at ground level. Churches, cars, and preconceptions can all become abstracted, safe protections against reality. Jesus himself spent a lot of time with common people and social outcasts in homes and public places. What he says about the poor, the powerless, and the oppressed demonstrates his familiarity with those persons and their circumstances.

Taking the plunge and going into the community can unveil your preconceptions and misconceptions. The members of your church may meet people they might never meet in church, and they may learn things about the community that they might never learn in Bible study. One initial way to break the ice is to assign five teams of two adventurous people each to walk through the community.

Walk the streets of your target area at different times during the day and night and also on a weekend. Pay attention to details. What do you see and hear? What kinds of people do you meet? Who frequents the shops and the agencies? What is missing? If you were a newcomer to the community, what would your impressions be?

Now that you have begun to get a feel for your community, in order to discover your ministry, you need to get a human and physical profile of the target area. You need to collect data on the population, housing, public services, and the businesses and industries that comprise the community. Three kinds of data are important to find:

1. Statistics on the present situation.
2. Changes that the present situation represents in relation to the past. (Comparative data indicate the social dynamics that are at work.)
3. Future projections made by government agencies or business interests.

Other sources of information that are available to the public include: census data[2]; surveys done by private business organizations; reports made by public agencies such as the police, welfare department, school board, planning office, and utility companies; local newspaper files; and university research work.

The purpose of gathering this kind of information is to construct an overall picture of the community and the pattern of social, political, and economic forces at work to shape its future.

Clues to the developmental patterns of your community can be found by exploring the following questions:

1. *Population profile.* What are the population percentages with regard to race, employment groups, and income levels? How have these percentages changed in the last ten years? What are the breakdowns by age, sex, family size, and types of living units?

2. *Life-cycle stage*. Is the community new, growing, stabilizing, changing, deteriorating? What is the condition of the housing and commercial property? What public services are provided? What are the value and number of owner-occupied homes, apartments, and condominiums? Are there slum areas?

3. *Economic base*. How many and what kind of businesses are located in your target area? Later in the process you will want to determine their ownership and employee locations, consider their effect on residential areas, and note the distribution and kinds of small businesses in your area.

4. *Community mood*. Does one political party dominate the local government? How are minority interests addressed? What emotions do people on the street reflect: pride, apathy, tension, intergroup conflicts, fear of crime, sense of well-being?

Identify the Organizations

After getting a general feel for how you perceive your community, you will want to begin to identify and assess the underlying foundation of the community. The voluntary social, religious, community, and business organizations are the "shadow government" of the community. Voluntarism and private initiative are fundamental to the American political system and the health of the community.

In preparation for planning your goals, you will want to know what issues are already being addressed by organizations present in the community. A first step is to review or compile a catalog of social service agencies and organizations which serve and/or are located in your target area. Next you will want to spend some time evaluating their effectiveness. You can begin by speaking to employees and clients to learn what they are actually doing. You may then want to compare their programs with their corporate goal statements. Are they doing justice by caring for the community, or are they catering to their private self-interests?

Interview Community Leaders

In order to obtain diverse perspectives on the community, it is important to interview leaders in fields like education, business and industry, government, communications, and social welfare, and to speak to leaders of minority groups.

The personal interview is used to get data from live sources. By doing personal interviews, you serve a twofold purpose: first, you are getting evaluations of how key leaders perceive the community; second, you are making it known to community leaders that your church is concerned about the needs and problems of the community.

In this project of discovering the developments, needs, and problems of the community, you may find that some leaders will be surprised at your interest and your desire to interview them. Demonstrate to them that you have no ax

to grind, but rather that you are seeking their expert help on how your church can care for the community.

Use your catalog of organizations to help you prepare your list of key leaders. You will also want to interview recipients of services. Some sample questions have been suggested in Appendix B. Each of your group members may choose to interview several persons on your list, or they may plan to go out in pairs. A practice session or role play will help less experienced members feel more confident. Plan a follow-up session for reporting back findings and experiences. Don't forget to send thank-you notes where appropriate.

Identify Community Decision Makers

To discover one's community means more than listing

the facts, issues, and needs of its residents. It also means discovering the decision makers within the community—the leaders that can make things happen.

Power is simply the capacity to act. The church that cares for its community through social service and social action is inevitably involved in the exercise of power—the power of the Holy Spirit and human organization. The church has moral authority where it speaks and acts for the kingdom of God in this society. When it acts on that authority by pressing for real social, political, and economic changes that will make this society more just, it becomes involved in the public exercise of power. In a democratic society the church has a constitutional right to be in the fight. In the gospel of the kingdom, the church has a moral responsibility to affect the way society is organized and run.

In every decision-making community there are people who exercise power. They are usually called community leaders, political leaders, or business leaders. Those who have been elected or appointed to office in government or the private sector are obviously people to know. In addition, there often are citizens who mold public opinion because they are charismatic persons who have found forums such as public meetings, events, organizations, and the media to put forth ideas and exercise personal authority.

The following are some kinds of leadership and levels of power to keep in mind when drawing "a people map" of the community:

1. *The social reformers or activists* are already involved in caring for the welfare of the community and trying to solve its problems. They are natural allies of the church planning to take a role in community affairs and they can be recruited for participation on some level.

2. *The opinion leaders* are personal authorities. They can sway public sentiment and thinking on issues. It is important to receive their blessing if not their support for a cause or at least to neutralize their opposition to what you are doing.

3. *The constituency* of social action are those people in the community most directly affected by the action you are taking, e.g., the victims of the injustice to be challenged and changed. Their involvement is essential to realism and inside knowledge about the problem being tackled by those advocating justice. (See Appendix C for help in organizing a needs assessment.)

4. There are two very different kinds of *experts*. One group is the *disciplined observers,* often academic types, who know the situation but are not involved in the social interaction as self-interested parties. They can serve as good resource people for community action. The other group is the *power brokers* who have a self-interest in the system affecting the constituency and stand to lose something if changes are made. They will serve as expert opponents of your cause.

Create a "Power Map"

A helpful way to visualize what you have learned is to lay out a chart giving an accurate power analysis of the community. The purpose of this "power map" is to save the local church from three common mistakes made by good-hearted people who enter the power struggle for justice. Those mistakes are: picking fights they cannot possibly win, naming the wrong opponents, and doing things that cannot cause any real change. Realism about power can make you more modest, more accurate, and more effective.

In order to understand how the community really works and who operates the levers of power in various spheres of influence, cover an eight-by-ten foot church wall with butcher paper that you can write on with marking pens. On this power map you will want to diagram three kinds of data gathered from your research efforts:

1. *Name all major organizations, agencies, institutions, and individuals* who influence the decisions being made about your community (i.e., everyone who has some power). That will include government, banks, insurance companies, utilities, real estate interests, businesses, churches, investors in all of the above, and so forth.

2. *Ring each name on the chart* with a larger or smaller circle, indicating an estimate of the amount of power that

person or institution wields in the community. This will be refined as you go along, and the actors will wield varying degrees of power on various issues/problems of the community.

3. *Make connections* by drawing lines between the names to indicate the relationships among actors. Then write in the precise nature of each "relational event" in terms of give-and-take, cooperation and opposition, money flows, friendship networks, business deals, and so forth. The real power brokers will emerge visually as many lines run to them, indicating their pivotal power positions.

The power map will serve as a strategic action planning tool on problem solving and community change by identifying the roles and relationships of the actors. Its cogency depends on figuring out *who is doing what to whom, and how and why they do it.*

Act Between Acts: Inter-Mission

If you have done the exercises suggested above in order to discover in depth the community you care about and you are faced with the realism such knowledge brings, *you may experience strong withdrawal symptoms.* The disparate data, the overwhelming and sometimes threatening experiences, and the painful insights may make you want to look for a way out of community involvement, or you may find yourself in one of these situations.

1. You may panic and want to return to the arms of the church community to do something familiar—like Bible study—among fellow believers. Since that is perfectly healthy for Christians, do it to clear your head and to open your mind to what is essential for the Christian community. (Turn to Appendix B for some suggestions for study.)

2. You may experience a bout with the dread disease known as "the paralysis of analysis syndrome." Here are some of the common symptoms identified by experienced clinicians: "We're not yet ready to act because we need

more information." "We need larger numbers and more talented people before we can act."

The inability to act is also shown in endless squabbling over alternative plans of action. An overload of information or action options can bring you to a halt that becomes a rationalization for doing nothing at all. The real bind may be the fear of risking any action at all. Admitting it and asking "why" is the first step out of powerless inertia.

3. You may decide to save the whole world while you are at it, not just the 79 welfare mothers and the 204 children. The way to play this withdrawal game is to generate a global goal so impossible you can never be held responsible for failing to achieve it. The task is to become fully human rather than playing God. To become serious about one limited local sign of the kingdom's nearness has more credibility than self-indulging Christian illusions of power and lordship that belong to Christ alone.

3
Identifying Areas of Community Concern

And Jesus went about all the cities and villages, teaching in their synagogues and preaching the gospel of the kingdom, and healing every disease and every infirmity (Matthew 9:35).

Data collection, learning, and an increasing understanding of the community are functions of caring and will continue as long as the church remains involved with the community. These skills will soon become a natural by-product of engagement rather than the academic exercise they may appear to be when starting up. Since community research is not an end in itself, evaluation and interpretation should follow closely on its heels. The question to be asked is, "What have we learned, and what does it mean for the mission of the church?"

Discovering the Issue

The local church needs to allow itself some time for the jobs of sifting, sorting, and integrating the research findings. The church can use all the skills its lay members have to do the task. They will need to piece together a picture of the community that offers functional and usable knowledge for deciding what the church will do to exercise its mission in the community. There are many ways to go about solving this puzzle. Here are some techniques that have proved helpful.

Strategic Scanning

Strategic scanning involves backing off in order to get a broad overview of the community. One integrates the detailed data in order to answer some basic questions:

1. *Stage*. What stage of the life cycle is this community experiencing—stability, improvement, decay?

2. *Trends*. What are the principal patterns of change in terms of population, buildings, services, businesses, and so forth?

3. *Actors*. Who are the key individual actors in the community and what are their objectives for community development? Which institutions and organizations have the greatest influence in shaping the community?

4. *Problems*. List the principal social problems of the community, the victims who experience each problem, and the perpetrators who cause the problems.

5. *Mood*. How do the people feel about their community? What are their expressed needs and hopes? What do they think about the role of your local church in the community?

Processing the Problems

The community research phase will probably bring to the surface far more problems than any single local church can or should address as part of its caring for the community. Unless some way is found to process the problems, the many human needs can lead either to inaction due to despair over being unable to solve them all, or to spreading resources so thin that no problem is really solved. Choices have to be made in order to stay sane and hopeful, and to be effective as a church.

The necessity to choose may present a moral dilemma for your community action group. How can one choose between equally urgent human needs? How can one trade off one kind of human suffering against another? There is no easy answer, but here are some ways to begin.

Problem Priority Scale

One way to process the community problems identified is to sort them out according to various factors such as their urgency, pervasiveness, numerical impact, attention they are now receiving, immediacy to your membership, and so forth. Using this process with moral sensitivity is one way to prioritize needs and thus choose the problems you should tackle. This is also a time to remember any priorities that have already been adopted by your church, association, or denomination.

Create a simple matrix grid and list the problems you have identified in the community across the top of the newsprint. Down along the left-hand side, list the critical factors you have chosen to weigh each problem listed.

PROBLEM PRIORITY SCALE[1]										
Problems Identified This problem is . . .	Weighting Factors used to determine Problem Priorities									
	1	2	3	4	5	6	7	8	9	10
1 . . . basic as a key to unlock other problems										
2 . . . urgent because of crisis/ suffering										
3 . . . neglected; no one is now working on it										
4 . . . widespread, involving many people										
5 . . . affecting some of our church members										
6 . . . local, but it also has a national impact										
7 . . . hardest on the poor and minorities										
8 . . . solved by personal service and charity										
9 . . . solved by changing policies and institutions										
10 . . . one that has a handle to grab onto										
11 . . .										
12 . . .										
TOTAL CHECK MARKS										
PRIORITY RATING										

Under each problem listed at the top, put a checkmark for each weighting factor that applies to it. Count the total number of checks in each case and compare the totals. Put the problems in priority order using these scores. Consider any other specifics that are important to your local church or your community.

Choose a Triad of Issues

Another way to process the community problems identified in the research is based on the following assumptions: (a) A local church cannot handle any more than three community problems at a time if justice is to be done to each one. (b) The social concerns adopted by a church should be a mix that includes:

1. Choosing one problem that has strong local manifestations and national or even global ramifications as an issue that affects the larger human community. This will enable you to experience the interlocking connections of some basic justice issues, to draw on wider church resources and organizations, and "to bring the issue home," so to speak.

2. Choosing one problem that involves your local church members directly with the poor, the powerless, and the oppressed members of the community. This will enable you to experience the justice issues from the hopeless bottom of society and to advocate the cause of the people Christ constantly directs us to in the Gospels.

3. Choosing one problem that grabs the local church members themselves where they may be smarting from injustice. This will enable you to experience the reality that we are all victims in some way in an unjust society, as well as victimizers who benefit from reigning social, political, and economic arrangements.

The process is simple to use but requires intuition, critical judgment, and moral sensitivity. Using the "Problem Priority Scale," or a list of issues and needs, discuss the choice of three problems that meet the previously outlined criteria.

Looking Ahead

We have been looking outward from the church building into the community which is one focus of the church's mission. We have discussed various techniques that a local church can use to get inside its community to find out how it works and who makes it work. Besides learning a lot of things, the objective has been to identify several problems that the church can work on in order to act out its concern for the community.

In the next two chapters we will look inward to discover the community of the local church, its present program, its resources, and prospects for social service and action in the world.

4

The Laity in Ministry

And he said to them, "The harvest is plentiful, but the laborers are few; pray therefore
the Lord of the harvest to send out laborers into his harvest" (Luke 10:2).

In the one church of Jesus Christ there is only *one gospel, one Lord, and one ministry.* That ministry is the way we Christians express our enthusiasm, commitment, and gratitude to the God who liberated us from darkness, sin, and death and raised us up whole, free, and alive again. That ministry is the way we live, work, share God's story, and our own story. It is what we do for others within and without the church. *Christian ministry is our whole style of living, loving, and serving.* Ministry is our Christian vocation, no matter what our occupations are.

Lately the Christian ministry has been carried out primarily by the professional clergy. It is time that lay persons reclaim their ministry as well!

Three things are clear about the one ministry of the church in the New Testament.

1. All baptized Christians—men, women and children—are Christ's ministers. Baptism is the ordination in which each one is set apart from the world and joined to Christ by the confession that Christ is Lord and Savior. There is no higher office, greater status, or more important discipleship in the church than the vocation of "plain Christian folks" given in baptism.

2. Some Christians were set aside for specialized functions in the church because they had gifts useful to the gathered community—like preaching, teaching, caring for the sick, controlling the finances, or cooking the common meals. They worked in the world as Christ's ministers like everyone else and were not "full-time church employees." It took centuries and fantastic church growth to evolve professional clergy.

3. In the New Testament, "to minister" means "to serve." The Greek word for it, "diakonia," is defined by the image of a table waiter who is a menial servant or slave (Luke 17:8). That is the image Jesus used to picture his vocation as the Messiah, one who "came not to be served

but to serve" in giving his life for many (Matthew 20:28, Luke 22:27). He took the form of a servant-slave (Philippians 2:5-11), and became a poor man in order to make us rich in love for others (2 Corinthians 8:9). The New Testament church identified itself as the body of Christ in this world until Jesus comes again. The church gathered in Jesus' image and pattern of life because he is the one and only head of the Christian community.

Each member of your congregation is responsible for naming and claiming his or her own ministry according to gifts, occupation, and the needs of the human community. There are *inreach ministries* like church worship, education, and managing the building and money of the church. There are also *outreach ministries* like evangelism, social service, and advocacy actions directed toward the wholeness and justice of the larger society.

While some were set apart to exercise special gifts of the Spirit in the early church, there was only one ministry with its various functions shared by the "laos," the laity or whole people of God. The church described in Acts exercised all of the gifts listed in the following chart, working together as a living embodiment of its Lord.

The ministry of the church in Acts was holistic, activistic, and socially involved in the secular world to a remarkable degree given its political and economic context. Remember, this church was outlawed, persecuted, and politically repressed in a totalitarian society. To get some feeling for the early church's courage, let's look at some contemporary churches in similar societies.

● In Poland, priests who support human rights and a democratic labor movement are murdered by a leftist police state because the kingdom of God is subversive to communist dictatorships.

● In El Salvador, nuns engaging in service ministries to the peasant poor are murdered by a rightest police state

Nurture, or Inreach	Gifts of the Spirit and Marks of the Church in Acts[1]	Mission, or Outreach
	Kerygma	
Preaching and teaching	Telling the story of God's salvation of the whole world in Christ	Evangelizing
	Diakonia	
Caring for brothers and sisters in faith: giving to the poor; supporting the sick, the infirm, and disabled; supporting widows and orphans; caring for missionaries and poor churches	Doing the truth in Christ	Caring for outsiders through social service and action: giving to the poor; supporting the sick, the infirm, and disabled; supporting widows and orphans; relieving disaster and famine; giving and getting work
	Koinonia	
Living together in the church through shared possessions, and fellowshiping across racial and class lines	Living the new community in Christ	Living together in the world
	Leitourgia	
Worshiping, celebrating agape feasts, burying the dead	Celebrating the gospel of Christ	Celebrating the world and its people as God's good creation

because the kingdom of God is dangerous to capitalist dictatorships.

• In South Africa, black Christians acting for a just society have no political rights and are economically enslaved by a white state because the kingdom of God does not tolerate racial oppression.

The early church with its economically and politically liberating gospel was a threat to the Roman Imperium. Christians were rightfully charged with atheism because they refused to recognize any ruler—whether it was Caesar, pharaoh, or any of the kings, premiers, presidents, and petty princes of this world—as God. When Jesus is Lord, there are no other lords to be obeyed, and there are no governments that can overrule his rule. In spite of the impossible situation, which would have justified a church turned in upon itself to concentrate on personal and private faith, members of the early church spoke and acted publicly for

their Lord and Savior. They demonstrated Christian courage and loyalty in the worst of circumstances.

In the United States our churches live in the best of circumstances. The United States is the oldest enduring democracy on the face of the earth. We're a free, open, constitutional republic that includes religious liberty as an inalienable human right in its charter. This society has more wealth, more natural resources, more power, and more humane political traditions than any other society that has ever existed.

Given our large national churches and an overwhelming Christian citizen majority, we can make this society a gem of justice in the Ruler's crown. We have a higher calling and a far better prospect of coming close to the kingdom of God in the United States than most of the other nations of the earth. Socially concerned churches are vital to the task.

5

Local Church Resources for Community Ministry

. . . you are a chosen race, the King's priests, the holy nation, God's own people, chosen to proclaim the wonderful acts of God, who called you out of darkness into his own marvelous light (1 Peter 2:9, TEV).

The little band of disciples that Jesus called to follow him were not great in number or prestige as the world counts greatness. Many were fishermen, some were businessmen—all were common folk. The thing that distinguished them from others was their response to Jesus' call and commissioning.

It is easy to think of yourself and your congregation as "just plain folks." Yet in a society where bigness and wealth are signs of success, a study by a large Protestant denomination reveals that 50 percent of its churches have less than 180 members. Another study reveals a 9 percent membership loss over the last decade. With images like these it is possible to conclude that "we're nobodies who have fewer and fewer bodies all the time, and there is nothing we can do about our creeping invisibility in this dark world."

On the other hand, numbers alone do not predict weakness. And some of those plain folks may possess gifts and skills as well as links to the community that can be used for a caring ministry. With a positive perspective and a conviction that the gospel is true and that Jesus has called you to discipleship, you can conclude that "we're some-

bodies in Christ's kingdom, and there is nothing we can't do as God's own people in this dark world."

You don't have to be important, you don't have to be big, and you don't have to be rich. However, you must have the courage to risk.

What Do We Have Going for Us?

You have much more going for you than you think or even dare hope if you haven't done a recent inventory of your assets and strengths as a local church. The first step is to identify and to affirm your distinctive resources as a congregation. Then imagine how each could be used to support and expand your community outreach. You will like what you are about to do because it is encouraging and empowering to be surprised by discovering gifts and blessings you didn't know you had or have taken for granted.

Asset Number 1: Member-Ministers Performing

Your church lay members are a human resource that is the most valuable asset you have. Each layperson has a vocation of service and action within God's kingdom. Both the richness of their gifts and skills and how they may exercise them in their community and church remain to be discovered. In order to do this, turn to Appendix G for two helpful exercises:

1. *Personal Gifts Inventory*—a tool which will enable each person in the congregation to identify what he or she has accomplished and the skills used in doing those things.

2. *Lay Ministries Inventory*—a tool that will identify all that your member-ministers are doing in the community beyond the programs sponsored by the local church.

When the congregational inventory of gifts is completed, it can be used in several ways. One way is to use it as a skills bank in order to match people with the kinds of jobs that need to be done in the church or the community. Another

way to use it would be to plan new community ministries using the untapped skills of the member-ministers of your congregation. Think what could happen if you put all this skilled people-power to work on some problems!

The social concerns group may want to communicate the findings by means of a map of the community showing all the involvements of member-ministers of the church. The data could also be entered on "the power map of the community" suggested in Chapter 2. Since it is important that people involved in this kind of exercise see the results as well as the reason for doing it, find a way to summarize and share the data with the whole congregation and have a celebration for the member-ministers.

One more encouraging word: *there is real power in people,* even in a small church! Many other organizations in the community would appreciate having a loyal membership as devoted and talented as yours. Remember that the power to achieve social change in any community requires two fundamental things: (a) intimate knowledge of the problems, and (b) a constituency organized to work for change. You already have the people, so now your task is organizing them and getting the knowledge needed to make a difference in your community. You're already halfway to empowerment right now!

Asset Number 2: Mission Accomplishments

Having assessed individual gifts and member-ministries, we will now turn to a discovery of what the congregation itself is doing. The question is, "What programs and services does your church offer persons and groups in the wider community?" Your social concerns group can list them on chalkboard or newsprint, trying to be as exhaustive as possible.

The second question to ask is, "How do you feel about what your church is doing in the community?" In order to answer this question, place a letter before each item you listed in answer to the first question. Ask each member of

the group to list the letters on paper and to rate each item on a scale of 1-10 ("10" denotes high enthusiasm, "5" denotes neutrality, and "1" means dissatisfaction). Express your honest evaluation of each item on the list of community ministries.

Ask each person to put his or her numerical ratings on the list. Total them for each item and divide by the total number of people participating in order to arrive at a score for each ministry. Then rank the list from most important to least important based on the group's evaluation.

You might also estimate the number of budget dollars and "people hours" the congregation puts into each ministry per year, and compare those expenditures with your priority ratings. Another comparison could be made between the ranked list of present community ministries and "the community problem priority scale" suggested in Chapter 3. Eventually, the question must be asked, "What does all this tell us about ourselves and our local church?"

You may be interested in where you stand in relation to what other congregations are doing in the community. For example, consider the results of a 1981 research sample of 248 churches of one denomination that were started since 1950.[1] In that sample, the church programs and services in the community were ranked as follows according to the number of churches engaged in each type of ministry on the list:

Community Programs and Services	Number Involved
1. Meeting space	145
2. Counseling	126
3. Hospital/nursing home visitation	108
4. Study/discussion	70
5. Music	53
6. Youth center	38
7. Emergency service	38
8. Prison visitation	35
9. Community action	34
10. Racial/ethnic understanding	30
11. Day care	28
12. Nursery school	28
13. Meals on wheels	17
14. Health care	12
15. Hot lunch	6

There was another interesting finding of that same research project. While some forms of service were more popular than others, church membership growth was correlated with two items: *community action* and *racial/ethnic understanding,* which were not ranked high on the scale.

Asset Number 3: Meeting Facilities

Offering church facilities as a meeting place for community groups and organizations was the most common service provided in the research sample noted above. Fully 58 percent of the churches were open to community use. One wonders why the other 42 percent were closed. This

"open door" service has definite benefits for a local congregation—

1. Gaining a reputation as a church that cares about the community and supports human initiatives;

2. Increasing church contacts with community leaders and organizations;

3. Getting new people through the doors for the first time.

By opening their doors, many urban churches have addressed the needs of working mothers, the hungry poor, the mentally handicapped, and community youth. A suburban church can house Boy and Girl Scouts, a chapter of the American Association of Retired Persons, Alcoholics Anonymous, Take Off Pounds Sensibly, or Parents Without Partners, or it can provide a neutral public forum for political candidates to debate the issues. Small-town and rural churches can find space for Red Cross Bloodmobiles, 4-H Clubs, the Grange, and similar worthy organizations.

A social concerns group will also realize the value of good public relations and free advertising for Christian or service ministries. For example, fifteen hundred people hear that the Weaver's Way Food Cooperative is holding its annual meeting of members in your church hall. They will learn the time, date, and place of their next meeting, and that this church cares for the whole community, not just its own members. They might also remember to attend a service there if they ever want to find a church home.

Asset Number 4: Money and Other Roots

The New Testament records numerous stories of God's ability to provide. Near the community of Bethsaida Jesus turned five loaves and two fish into a feast to feed five thousand in need. Financial resources for ministry can be a "sign" of God's presence, and when shared freely they may be used by God to create modern miracles.

Here is a super sign that is simple for your local church

to do. Take your two biggest special offerings of the church year—the Christmas and Easter offerings—and give them away. Give them in equally divided shares to five organizations in the community doing things you can connect with the work or words of Jesus. Give them to groups such as:

● The local shelter for the homeless, or the shelter of the Salvation Army. Christ also had nowhere to lay his head.

● The nonprofit medical clinic that charges those who "have" and heals the "have-nots" free. Christ healed the sick regardless of their ability to pay.

● The refuge for abused women and children who bear in their bodies the pain of our social and economic brutalities. Christ spoke against human violence; we can help its victims.

● The peace activists and nuclear disarmament groups at whatever church or churches involved in these programs in your area. Christ's body is not divided into denominations, nor dismembered by the wars of nations.

● The educational program that trains high school dropouts, and provides them with skills employable on today's job market. Christ was also called "Rabboni," teacher.

Give it all away. Give away your two best opportunities to increase your income. Give it away for the sake of others in need in the community. Give it away as a sign of God's presence which will amaze those within and without the church. Give it away and your own church budget baskets will also be filled. Wonders alone beget wonders of faith in the kingdom of God. Jesus came doing wonders, and so can you.

(P.S. If you cannot find the above types of organizations in your community, enlarge your definition of community.)

Asset Number 5: The Message

If people ask why your church gave $7,000 to five community organizations, you may simply want to tell them that it was because of Christmas and Easter. If they show some confusion about the meaning of those festivals, you may want to tell them the story of the five loaves and two fish. Or tell them the whole gospel story.

Never tell more than people are ready to hear. Listen to them first, and demonstrate the message by telling actions as well as words.

God is already present in you as a sign of power. God is already the Word in action to those who have eyes to see and ears to hear. God is free and serves as God's own witness. Our human words can only point obliquely to God's Word and Deed in Jesus Christ present among us here and now.

This is our Christian witness. *We never are the gospel; never own it; never possess it; and never control it.* We are only authorized to act on it and to name the One who is present in the human events that take place. In action, the church speaks loudly and clearly. Words without actions are empty, and actions without words are blind.

Asset Number 6: The Minister Called Reverend

As a representative of a group of concerned lay people in the congregation, invite your pastor to lunch and share with him or her three things:

1. We propose that our congregation make social ministry a program priority for the next three years, and reorganize our resources to begin acting on one critical social issue in the community.

2. We propose that the gifts, knowledge, and experience required for acting on the issue are to be found primarily in the laity who will take major responsibility for the social ministry.

3. We propose that you, our clergyperson, provide strong pastoral leadership and support for the social ministry and skillfully manage the conflict it may cause in the congregation.

Measuring the kind of response and the feeling level of the clergy will give you some idea of the prospects for the program. The pastor is a crucial person in the social ministry.

Research done on congregations indicates that social action programs rarely get off the ground without strong clergy leadership as well as lay support. This is especially true in the initial stages. (Lay leadership becomes the most important operational factor once the ministry is under way.)

Your clergyperson will be either your first ally or the first person you will have to convert to a social concerns endeavor of the local church. Then he or she will be one of your best resources and a very important asset, not only to the lay social ministry but also to your local church growth. Research also shows that certain specific clergy skills correlate positively with membership growth. *The five primary skills shown by the clergy in growing churches are:*[2]

- Social issue activity
- Managing conflict
- Teaching
- Evangelizing
- Preaching

Asset Number 7: Memories That Are Promises

Eli Weisal has said that a person with no history is poorer than a person who has no future.

Traditions are important because they tell us who we are as well as who we have been. *Tradition is essential to identity. It contributes to continuity.* It offers a golden thread that can be traced and an evolving story that prepares one for a future different from the present and the past. Socially concerned congregations usually develop a rich tradition that has three components.[3]

A Usable Local Church History

You cannot change the past or fabricate your church's history, but *you can rediscover and reinterpret it* from contemporary perspectives. History is rather like Ambrose Bierce's comment on saints. He said, "Saints are Christians . . . revised and edited!"[4] So is history edited in the writing; for example, women who were edited out of the story are being rediscovered as today's women tell their stories with new consciousness.

Your local church history should be searched for all the events, actions, and statements which can be used to undergird your social ministry. This can be done by asking questions like these: What were the social problems of the community during the first fifteen years after the founding of the church? How did the founders respond to them? What about later periods? What justice issues has the congregation addressed locally or in the nation in the past?

The faithfulness of another generation can both inspire and challenge us today as we remember who we were and are, and as we think about who we can be in the future.

The Biblical Tradition Recalled

The most important single voice in the church is the Bible itself—rich in stories, events, and words from the Lord that ratify and even command a social ministry on behalf of justice in society. Use Bible stories because they are true and have maximum power and authority in the church.

Socially concerned congregations will naturally gravitate to prophetic passages in both testaments and stories of the people of God in action, movement, and change. Current study and interpretation of the Exodus, Law, Covenant, Exile, Suffering Servant, and the New Covenant can direct and support the congregation's initiatives in social concerns. As those revealing biblical events shape your life as a congregation, they will become an integral part of your story today and provide the controlling images for your own identity and purpose.

An Oral Tradition Celebrated

Socially concerned congregations usually create an ongoing narrative and conversation that is central to their life. It expresses their self-perception as a congregation unique in its style and ministries. Their "song or lore" tells their story of relating to the larger society through their mission.

In biblical terms, this narrative is their "wisdom tradition" of learnings and is often associated with events in their life—cherished people and memories, triumphs, and disasters. These are recalled and retold both because they are enjoyed and because they provide insights for current problems and decisions of the community.

Some congregations actually write songs about their life and develop curriculum pieces for children or orientation materials for new members that tell their story of social ministry. They believe they have a significant history and learnings to pass on to others, and they do. Much of the Bible once was this same kind of oral tradition.

Count All Your Assets

We have suggested seven assets that you have as a congregation. Several are collective, as in the case of your member-ministers, and count more like seventy times seven. Large or small, your congregation is beautiful and full of empowered people. Any problem in "coming alive" is probably not due to a lack of assets but a matter of liberating frozen assets. Be of good courage, . . . "You will know the truth, and the truth will make you free" (John 8:32).

6

Four Arenas of Community Ministry

"Truly, truly, I say to you, he who believes in me will also do the works that I do; and greater works than these will he do, because I go to the Father" (John 14:12).

"But you shall receive power when the Holy Spirit has come upon you; and you shall be my witnesses in Jerusalem and in all Judea and Samaria and to the end of the earth" (Acts 1:8).

When Jesus was about to empower the new young church by the Holy Spirit, he envisioned that its ministry would be an ever-widening and ever-growing one. By the end of the book of Acts the gospel had reached as far as Rome, and in the modern era the gospel has been translated into thousands of the world's languages and dialects. It has influenced the course of nations, the worlds of the arts and sciences, and the welfare of the human race to a degree the first disciples could never have imagined! As the world has grown larger and more complex, so have the need, the opportunity, and the means for Christian caring. Nowhere is this more true than in the neighborhoods and communities which surround our churches!

Arenas of Community Caring

Following is one model of organizing for caring and change toward a more just society. The diagram includes four distinct arenas of community action for church mission outreach. These arenas *are not exclusive of one another.* Several at a time may be used by a church that is working on more than one issue in the community. Nor is one arena necessarily better than another since each can be recommended in different situations. A church that is strong on social concerns may be involved in all at the same time, or make more than one response to the same basic issue.

The chart names the four optional arenas of caring for the community as a congregation. It begins on the lower left with *social service* and moves around through increasingly complex kinds of organization and uses of power to the point of *public policy action* where one is dealing with the governance of society itself. Sectors 1, 2, and 3 are usually called "the private sector," where voluntary associations and business organizations operate. Sector 4 is "the public sector," where the civil authority functions on behalf of all citizens.

In order to describe and compare the four approaches a congregation may take, we will deal with each one in more detail.

Social Service

Social service is the *church provision of immediate and direct aid to individuals or groups who are hurting or have unmet basic human needs.* This lay ministry may take the form of food cupboards, shelters, relief money, job education, health care or day care, rehabilitation, resettlement, or personal crisis intervention, among others. Social service is the most obvious, accepted, and traditional way to care for needy people in the community and is widely accepted as a legitimate and faithful form of Christian social ministry.

Social service is as old as the church. Jesus' community first lived a simple life of sharing resources, healing, and supporting the needs that surprised the public and threatened the governors (Acts 3–4). Jesus imagined the last judgment of nations and religions turning on services provided to "the least of these" (Matthew 25:31ff). He answered the question about his messiahship with, "Go and tell John what you have seen and heard: the blind receive their sight, the lame walk, lepers are cleansed, and the deaf hear, the dead are raised up, the poor have good news preached to them" (Luke 7:22). Jesus' judgment of social service as love of both God and neighbor will remain valid until Judgment Day.

No one dares put genuine social service down as "mere charity" or a "Band-Aid operation" when it is done in love and without paternalism, power games, proselytizing, or pride. It has gotten a bad name because of abuses by evangelists who fish for souls by baiting their hooks with bread, by the very wealthy who attend charity balls in designer gowns costing $5,000, and by governments that buy peasant political support with sacks of surplus wheat.

Four Arenas of Church Outreach
Through Community Caring and Social Change[1]

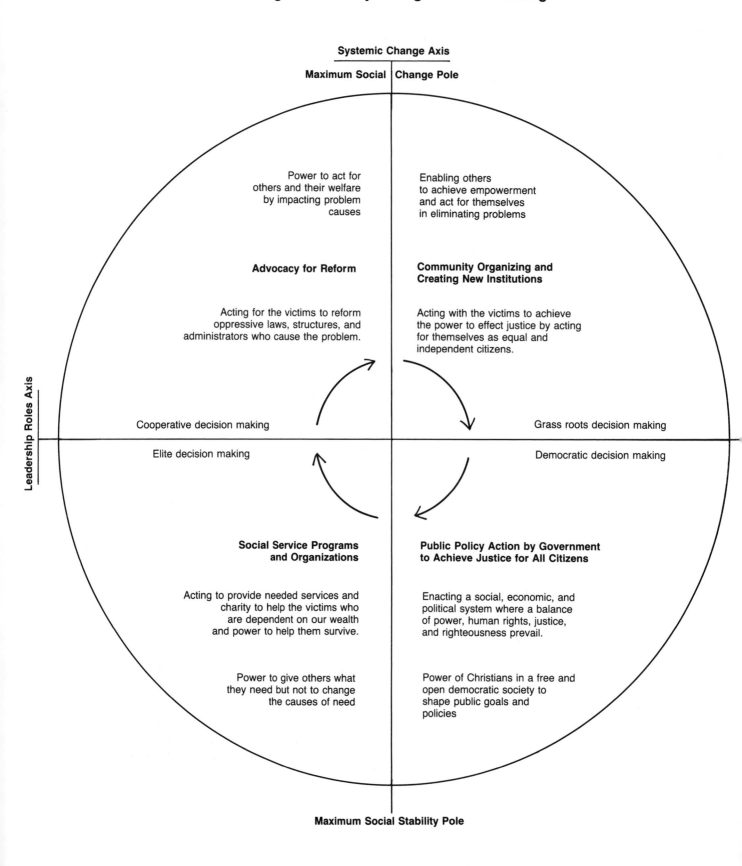

Systemic Change Axis

Maximum Social | Change Pole

Power to act for
others and their welfare
by impacting problem
causes

Enabling others
to achieve empowerment
and act for themselves
in eliminating problems

Advocacy for Reform

**Community Organizing and
Creating New Institutions**

Acting for the victims to reform
oppressive laws, structures, and
administrators who cause the problem.

Acting with the victims to achieve
the power to effect justice by acting
for themselves as equal and
independent citizens.

Leadership Roles Axis

Cooperative decision making

Grass roots decision making

Elite decision making

Democratic decision making

**Social Service Programs
and Organizations**

**Public Policy Action by Government
to Achieve Justice for All Citizens**

Acting to provide needed services and
charity to help the victims who
are dependent on our wealth
and power to help them survive.

Enacting a social, economic, and
political system where a balance
of power, human rights, justice,
and righteousness prevail.

Power to give others what
they need but not to change
the causes of need

Power of Christians in a free and
open democratic society to
shape public goals and
policies

Maximum Social Stability Pole

Social service does have its limits as well as its virtues. The limits are given here not to detract from direct, personal ministries of love, but to show how love must lead to larger issues of justice in a society.

1. Social service intends to liberate people from their present miserable conditions of suffering. It usually does so on the basis of an urgent crisis that is met by giving what is essential under the circumstances without trying to identify causes and culprits. It is a very good emergency style of ministry.

2. Social service works best with the *bad effects* of a social problem on the individuals and does not deal with the *basic causes* of the problem or the institutions involved. It aids the victims without being able to reach the social policies and people victimizing those who suffer. In fact, there is a possibility that the service can never be ended because both the oppressed and their oppressors may become dependent on such aid—the one in order to survive and the other to escape moral responsibility.

3. Social service is a natural way for Christians to begin working on a problem because it is a real mercy, offers firsthand experience and immediate rewards, breaks out of apathy, and makes a commitment to caring. One is doing something for the least of Jesus' brothers and sisters. Social service also leads naturally to doing more than emergency aid, such as looking for ways to stop the production of the specific suffering you are healing.

Some people make a distinction between *social service* and *social action*. While the division is not neat and the lines are not hard and fast, there are some practical differences in perspective and scope. The following chart sets them side by side. Each discipline has its own integrity.

Social Service	Social Action
1. engages in social charity work	1. engages in social change work
2. focuses on the hurting individuals and the effects social problems have on them	2. focuses on the hurtful institutions and the causes of social problems
3. acts on the victims	3. acts for and with the victims
4. may create dependence	4. fosters independence
5. deals with immediate challenges and crises	5. deals with pervasive problems and systemic conditions
6. works through a simple, direct kind of caring called ''love'' in the Bible	6. works through a more complex and compromised kind of social love called ''justice'' in the Bible

Caution: This is not an either/or choice (social service or social action) to be made since a church can do both as part of its ministry of caring for the community.

Advocacy for Reform

''Why should Christian[s] . . . wear out their strength in curing the effects of the evil and have no word about the evil itself?''[2]

Advocacy means speaking and acting on behalf of people who are hurting by holding accountable and seeking to reform oppressive structures, institutions, laws, and administrators. One becomes an ally and a defender of defenseless people, pleading their case for justice before those who have the power to make a difference. Advocacy assumes that the system is basically sound but needs renewal and the elimination of abuses in order to stop exploitation.

Advocacy for reform means that the church finds its voice, its courage, and its power to protest injustices until changes are made. The advocate identifies with the victims, identifies the causes of their suffering, and identifies changes that have to be made.

There is a big step from charity to identification with and intercession for the outsiders. It takes more love to work in solidarity with powerless people than it does to be a protected and privileged benefactor. It takes more risk to move against the stream of power and vested interests in society than it does to go with the flow. It takes respect to *act with and for* disadvantaged people in fighting injustices rather than *acting on* them in elitist style.

Below are three basic characteristics of advocacy action for *social change:*

1. *Advocacy action works primarily on changing the structures of society rather than changing individuals,* though such conversions can happen in the process as well. That means dealing with boards, committees, agencies, and institutions—those groups that *run* corporate life—and with their policies, regulations, and laws. This emphasis on corporate human practices is based on the assumptions that groups shape their members far more powerfully than members shape their groups, and corporate entities have a mind and logic of their own and are capable of far more power

and greater inhumanities than the individuals who serve them. Sin at its worst is usually embodied in the corporate and collective structures of society.

2. *Advocacy action is a deliberate and organized effort to alter community structures* in order to eliminate a problem and free those caught in it. Society is run by human beings and human institutions. With effort, one can usually lay a hand on the human sources of the problem who have power to make changes. Group advocacy is usually more effective than individual initiatives because there is more power in numbers. *Advocacy action tries to restore some balance of power for the sake of justice and reconciliation in society.* A good test of the justice of social policies is their impact on the social groups who have no power, few dollars, and little representation in the arenas where the policies are decided. What happens to the disadvantaged and "the least people" is a good test. Injustice feeds on the powerless.

Community Organization and the Creation of New Institutions

The third arena of church outreach is involvement in community organization. *The technique is to build a new, indigenous organization that includes existing community groups which join together in order to further common interests.* The purpose is empowerment, problem solving, development, and fair treatment by the political and economic structures of the city. It often begins with a *collaboration* to obtain better delivery of services, develops working *coalitions* on problems, and results in the creation of a new *community institution.*

Most communities will encompass a loose and isolated array of human associations: neighborhoods, local churches, public interest organizations, fraternal societies, small businesses, agencies, trade unions, private organizations, and ethnic and racial groups. What a community organizer does is to build a broad-based organization to which all of these diverse associations can belong and work together. It is "an organization of organizations," so to speak.

The key is community empowerment through knowledge, "troops," and strategic actions that enable the community to negotiate with the power interests and institutions. Two kinds of power structures primarily shape the life of the city: the political structures, and the economic structures whose activities, wealth, and property yield tremendous power as seen in real estate developers, banks, bond holders, the media, manufacturers, and merchants. Wealthy families and corporations often actually make the real decisions about a city through their influence and investments rather than through the local government. The community organization deals with this "shadow government" and power brokers who never stand for election to office.

The local church that initiates or participates in a community organization must develop skills and styles that are

largely foreign to the church—status as one among equals; the pursuit and exercise of power; the ability to build a secular organization; use of alliances and coalitions; and engagement in public issues, controversies, systemic problems, and social activism. It takes a mature laity to understand community organizing as Christian service in the world.

Public Policy Action by Government to Achieve Justice for All Citizens

A fourth style of Christian outreach takes place in *the arena of governance, law, and public policy.* One steps out of the voluntary sector into the public sector where social policies are backed by the enforcement powers of the state.

In this sphere, one piece of legislation by Congress or one decision by a president or mayor can undergird or undo all the social welfare work of all the voluntary organizations combined. Our tremendous public wealth plus the civil powers to tax, to legislate, and to enforce the laws make the public sector a testing ground of the humanity and values of our society.

This realism about public power does not denigrate Christian charity at all. It only suggests that Christian love must uphold one of the basic rules of love's justice: to whom much power is given, of him or her much will be required by the God who demands justice in human life. The church does not run this society nor is it responsible for its injustices. It is government that rules—the church rightly holds government responsible for the righteousness of its laws and policies. The church is the conscience of the nation.

As Christians we are free to be that national conscience. Life, liberty, and the free exercise of religion are among our inalienable rights. The U. S. Constitution protects not only our freedom to believe and to worship and our freedom to act on those beliefs personally, but also our freedom to act politically in the democratic process in order to institute or alter legislation and policies in ways informed by our Christian beliefs.

However, in our free society, in being the nation's conscience we must adhere to the rules. One rule is *the separation of church and state*. This rule was originally instituted *against government* in order to prevent the civil authority from showing religious favoritism, controlling religion, or establishing an official state religion. The popular mind has turned separation back *against the church* by saying that religion should have nothing to say or do with government, as if Caesar had an inalienable, divine right to rule. Even worse, some Christians say people of faith have neither the right nor the duty to become involved in secular public affairs, as if Caesar were god of the world.

The second rule is *one Christian, one vote*. Competition is the other side of the separation. Churches must compete with all other interests and institutions for the soul of the nation. In this we have an even chance. Individually and collectively we have all the necessary rights to carry out advocacy actions in the public arena. The American democratic experiment works through a system of checks and balances among competing self-interest groups who use power to further their own welfare and values through public policies. The church must compete in order to effect change in this system.

After we elect representative government, the third rule is that *policy decisions are made through the political process*. This includes public opinion, lobbying through hearings, visits, letters, watchdog and pressure groups, informed positions on public issues, demonstrations, media exposure, and so forth. Groups that do their homework, get involved, and express their views can have an ethical impact on public policies. Such public service is a lay Christian ministry in which our members enter the struggle to distribute public resources fairly and to hold government responsible for the public good.

Individual Christians can do anything political, but the church itself is limited in what it can do in its own name by the fourth rule: *A local church cannot endorse a candidate for public office, contribute to his or her campaign, or spend more than 5 percent of its resources in formal lobbying*. To do so will endanger the tax-exempt status of the church which is a benefit of a church/state separation and an important part of religious freedom.

Seen positively, up to $5,000 of your annual local church budget of $100,000 can be spent on hard-nosed lobbying activities without offending the IRS. The real problem is church fear of engaging in controversy over public issues, the desire to be "purely religious," and the denial that Christian values have any merit as grounds for organizing society. Into the ethical vacuum created by the silent, private church there step the narrow self-interest groups, the big corporations, the media, and big government who will control our Christian lives according to their values and benefits.

There is one other important form of governance in this society which is private but massive enough to have quasi-public effects for good or ill: the large business corporation. While privately owned and run for private profit, the big businesses also have corporate social responsibilities according to the churches who care about economic justice, the use of earth resources, and world peace. If government is not God, neither is Union Carbide, AT&T, IBM, Lockheed, Rockwell, Hanna Mining, or Bank of America.

If your church has endowment or capital funds invested, members who are managers or directors of corporations, or members who invest in the stocks and bonds market, your church has a stake in how some corporations are run and what they do to this society. We can make judgments about the social impact of a corporation's means of production and methods of commerce through inquiries, stockholder meetings, buying or selling, and even litigation. A socially concerned church can address a corporation concerning the human effects of its policies and practices.

These are not new methods. Some churches have long refused to invest in companies that produce liquor, tobacco, or arms. Today the church's list of social injuries and injustices has been brought up to date to include:

1. Pollution and destruction of the environment,
2. Discrimination on the basis of race or sex in employment, training, and promotion practices,
3. Excessive reliance on militarism,
4. Foreign investments under governments that repress the political and economic rights of large groups of citizens, and
5. Fraudulent marketing practices and the production of goods or services that are harmful to civilians or consumers.

There is much the church can do in all the arenas of community caring and social change. However, the church's action must include caring and change toward a more just society. It must deal compassionately with the needs of persons and groups who have been excluded for one reason or another from the basic benefits and opportunities of our society. But the church must also act for change in the social structures and systems that exclude, exploit, or oppress the vulnerable and the powerless in our communities. That is what Jesus said he was about in Luke 4:18-19:

> "The Spirit of the Lord is upon me,
> because he has anointed me to preach good news to the poor.
> He has sent me to proclaim release to the captives
> and recovering of sight to the blind,
> to set at liberty those who are oppressed,
> to proclaim the acceptable year of the Lord."

In his Spirit and by his power the church can do no less.

Before we consider ways to identify, define, and focus action on community justice issues, we will look at how one community made a difference by organizing for caring action.

7

How ONE Community Organized for Caring Action

"Which is easier, to say to the paralytic, 'Your sins are forgiven,' or to say, 'Rise, take up your pallet and walk'? But that you may know that the Son of man has authority on earth to forgive sins"—he said to the paralytic—"I say to you, rise, take up your pallet and go home." And he rose, and immediately took up the pallet and went out before them all; so that they were all amazed and glorified God, saying, "We never saw anything like this!" (Mark 2:9-12).

The ceiling in our dining room fell down. When it rains, there's water all over the dining room floor. We're really cold. We don't have any heat or warm water." The young girl's face was dirty, and her clothes were picked-over remnants from thrift-shop shelves, but her voice was clear and strong as she talked about her home in this large midwestern city. "We used to live in that building over there," she continued, pointing to the vacant building next door, "but we moved out this winter. Now there are huge rats in it." She lives with her mother and eight brothers and sisters in a six-room apartment. It costs $185 per month out of their welfare check, a check her mother seldom sees because the landlord intercepts it.

Helping People Gain a Sense of Control over Their Lives

Their story is echoed again and again in the slum areas of large cities where lavish homes have aged into dilapidated apartment buildings, halfway houses, and vacant lots. "In the inner city such as this," a community leader explains, "there are many people who feel they have little control over what happens to them. They need to be helped to see that they can make a difference in their lives, that change *is* possible, and that by banding together people can pressure the powers-that-be to make community systems more just. It's part of the Christian mission, as well as the essence of democracy, that people exercise their God-given right and responsibility to address community needs and work for greater justice."

Identifying with the Neighborhood

In the late 1960s, Ernest Christian accepted the call to become an associate pastor of a main-line church in an inner-city area. Sensitized by the civil rights movement of that decade, he had become involved in the federal gov-

ernment's Office of Economic Opportunity community action programs in the small city from which he was about to move. Faced with the decision of where to reside in the new city to which he had been called, he chose to move his family into a church-owned residence in the neighborhood in order to identify with the church's community.

The church's immediate neighborhood was made up of middle-class families living in large, older, well-maintained homes, many of them built by their ancestors. In the course of getting to know his new neighbors, the recently arrived minister discovered a group who were interested in reviving a residents' council organized by an earlier generation to preserve the residential character of the neighborhood. The new residents' council, however, was envisioned to be more than a preserver of property values; it was to be open to all neighborhood residents and to be aimed at developing a genuine sense of community.

It so happened that, during the reorganization of the residents' council, the church trustees proposed that one of the church's residential properties in the neighborhood be razed to make way for a parking lot for its suburban commuters. Since a property use change required a zoning variation, including Zoning Board action and neighbor notification, the church and neighborhood were on a collision course. The issue for the residents' council was that if they permitted this particular zoning variation, what precedent would be set for other nonresidential uses, such as, for example, a service station? Ernest found himself pleading with the church for greater sensitivity to its neighbors and pleading with the neighborhood for recognition of the church's efforts to minister to children and youth in the area. The residents agreed to continue letting church members park on neighborhood streets, and the church withdrew its plans for a variation and sold the property to a new owner who continued to develop it as a residence.

Responding to Broader Community Needs

The visibility afforded Ernest by his neighborhood mediating role led to his election, first as a board member and then as president of a community council embracing an area of the city comprising about sixty thousand persons. This community council had developed three particularly strong service programs. One was a building conservation program which employed a retiree of a utility company to monitor residential and commercial properties and encourage owners to maintain their buildings and their surroundings. A second was an emergency food and clothing center staffed by trained volunteers who counseled clients regarding the availability of welfare services for long-term needs. This program was heavily supported by churches in the community through food, clothing, and financial contributions, as well as volunteers. A third program encouraged community residents to purchase and wear about their necks a whistle which could be used to summon help for themselves or their neighbors if victimized by crime. The Whistlestop program was of particular interest to the elderly, who felt the most vulnerable on the streets of the community. The program eventually spread to other parts of the city and nation.

Dealing with Root Causes

The difficulty with these programs was that, as effective as they were in responding to some of the symptoms of community problems, they did not address the underlying causes. What were the major factors contributing to building deterioration, rampant poverty, and crime on the streets? With the help of a professional community organizer, community leaders came together to explore that question. In addition to Ernest as community council president, the group included a director of a major social service agency, the director of a Hispanic community social service center, a staff member of the state administration, the pastor of a prominent Presbyterian church, the president of a minority contractors association, and two respected leaders of neighborhood grass-roots organizations. This group reached the conclusion that the need was for an organization of organizations that would cut across community boundaries and unite a variety of constituencies while preserving the racial, ethnic, and economic diversity of its two large inner-city communities. The area targeted was a major "port of entry" to the city for persons of almost every ethnic origin. The area's central high school at one point included students from thirty-nine of the United States and sixty-four foreign countries from every major continent!

The first step in the organizing process was bringing together a broadly representative group of leaders of organizations who shared the core group's vision and were willing to engage in action to demonstrate that community change was both possible and achievable. Action groups were formed around a number of community concerns—

economics, education, justice, land use, and housing. Interested citizens were invited to participate in issue research, strategy, and action.

Making Progress on Important Issues

Significant victories were won on major community issues. Reinvestment agreements were negotiated with local

financial institutions to counter the redlining[1] which plagued the community. The banks agreed to report, first by zip code and later by census tract, their lending activity in the community and to set measurable targets for reinvestment. This was the first such agreement in the nation achieved by a community organization. In another instance, minority contractors were enabled through negotiations with the state to enter into joint ventures with major contractors in the construction of a multimillion-dollar community college. The contracts resulted in additional community employment for minority persons as well as additional dollars for the community's economy.

Community leaders also made certain that the curriculum of the new community college would include vocational and technical skills important to community employment opportunities.

In the area of justice the state's attorney was persuaded to open a branch office in the community to bring his services closer to the people, a probation office was established to deal with the adult probationers in the area, and the city was pressured to break up large police districts and assign ethnic officers to relate to the special needs of the diverse community.

As a direct result of a new state policy to decentralize mental health care, 72 percent of the city's after-care beds (including halfway houses and nursing homes) had become concentrated in a single area of the city. The situation led to the "warehousing" of such needy persons in former apartment hotels and similar buildings. The deterioration of care was due to overburdened community facilities and services, as well as an excessive "institutionalization" of the community. The city department of health was persuaded to change the basis of its certificate of need policy from a city-wide to an area-by-area determination. This change enabled other city areas to participate more equitably in the accommodation and care of mental health patients.

Developing Community Involvement and Accountability

The challenges and successes of the actions greatly broadened community participation. A biennial convention was formed to which the various organizations of the community sent delegates to determine action areas and issues. The participating organizations included churches, community councils, school councils, residents' councils, block clubs, business associations, and service organizations. Out of these conventions have come positions on a wide range of community issues that are pursued through volunteer action groups until they are resolved. Even when a problem isn't totally resolved, the involvement of people in working toward neighborhood improvement is, in itself, a major accomplishment. The organization functions with a small staff of experienced community organizers who provide training and back-up assistance to community volunteers. Funding comes from delegating groups, community fund-raising activities, denominations, foundations, and other agencies committed to community improvement and change.

Taking Christian Responsibility for Community Change

Many of the volunteers who provide leadership for this community organization are members of the congregations of various religious traditions—Catholic, Protestant, and Jewish. Their motivation for involvement in the community organizing effort is their commitment to the Judeo-Christian concern for persons and a vision of the kingdom of God that includes caring for the community and doing justice.

Their values were highly instrumental in shaping the organization's lofty goal: "ONE (The Organization of the North East) is committed to maintaining the diverse ethnic and economic nature of the Uptown and Edgewater communities, to effectively promoting the dignity of all their people, and to the community determination of solutions to problems." The acronym ONE speaks for itself!

The next two chapters are designed to help with organizing for caring community action.

8
Gearing Up to Respond

[The] great stumbling block . . . is the [Christian] moderate . . . who prefers a negative peace which is the absence of tension to a positive peace which is the presence of justice. . . . In the midst of a mighty struggle to rid our nation of racial and economic injustice, I have heard so many ministers say, "Those are social issues with which the gospel has no real concern. . . ."[1]

At this point you have accomplished the basic groundwork for church action in the community by looking at the two principal components involved. You have researched the secular community and its problems (Chapter 2) and you have assessed your own local church involvement and its resources for community change (Chapters 3 and 5). That puts you in a position to bring the church and community together in a plan of action that matches your abilities and the needs of others.

We will pick up the process at the point where you have already identified the problems of the community and have chosen three of them as priorities for your community concern.

Define One Problem to Work On

One has to begin somewhere. Beginnings are always hard but are often made easier if the social concerns group can be *concrete, specific, and definite* about the problem it is going to tackle. Someone once said, "God is in the particulars." That is exactly what the incarnation says about God in Jesus Christ and why the gospel speaks of fallen sparrows

noticed and hairs counted, and gives the names of people healed.

Action requires specificity. Even after you have identified three problem priorities and have chosen one to begin working on, that one still has to be framed simply and concretely. Identifying a problem only in general terms like crime, slums, poverty, jobs, drugs, and so forth will frustrate and confuse people unless problems are transformed into specifics that are *vivid, manageable, and alive.* It is time to name names!

Here are two exercises that you may want to use in order to move from the general to the particulars in defining the problem.

Exercise 1: Touch-In with Four Informed People

Talk to people who can speak about the problem with some experience of it or authority on it. You may not have encountered them during the community research phase and, if not, it is now imperative that you find and consult them on the problem you have owned as your own. The four persons you need to talk to are:

● A *victim* of the problem who experiences what happens to people.

● An *outside advocate* of the victims who is involved with trying to solve the problem.

● An *expert* on the problem who knows about it through research or experience.

● A *decision maker* who has the power to do something about the problem because of ownership, responsibility, or office.

Exercise 2: Boil the Problem Down to One Sentence

Simplicity is a gift of the Spirit and a mark of genius or childlikeness. Many public problems are submerged in rhet-

oric, confused debate, and dead ends. After all, somebody is getting hurt, others are benefiting, and somebody should do something about it—but nothing is happening.

If you are going to effect change, you must have *a clear, concise, and cogent definition of the problem*. In order to achieve it, use the discipline of putting it in a one-sentence statement that names the following:

- *Subject:* who is doing or not doing something.
- *Verb:* what the subject is doing or not doing.
- *Predicate:* the object or to whom it is happening.
- *The Consequences:* the end result of it all.

For example, "The Claim-Jump Realty Company buys homes in Germantown at sheriff sales and milks them for high profits until they are slum buildings."

The definition of the problem is important because your presentation of the problem will show how much you actually know about it, support is more easily enlisted for concrete problems, and it gives your social concerns groups a specific place to start organizing.

As you get into the problem more deeply, the definition will become even more specific and the one sentence will grow into a complete analysis based on the beginning thesis statement. For example, who is the subject, "Claim-Jump Realty Company?" Who owns the corporation or partnership? How many properties do they own, where are they located, and in what condition are they? How does this organization get around city licensing and inspection and get away with building code violations? What contributions do they make to which political campaigns?

Find the Issue Focus for Action

In broad terms, we are following a progression of steps that map out like this:

—Discover Areas of Concern
—Define the Problem
—Choose Your Issue
—Determine the Action Objective
—Prepare Operational Plans
—Choose Your Tactics
—Move Into Action
—Celebrate
—Evaluate

The precise definition of the problem is necessary along with the knowledge needed to frame it because in the process *an actionable issue* will emerge. Research, prayer, and fasting may produce the issue as a gift of the Spirit to your social concerns group. *An issue is a handle where you can take hold of the problem.* (For example, why are the city building codes not being enforced in the case of Claim-Jump Realty properties?) An issue is some part of the problem that can be grabbed because it is symbolic of the whole problem. Confronting an issue is a way for you to take the initiative for the first time and make the world respond to you. In taking an issue on, you shift from reaction to pro-action by intervening to exert some power and begin the process of change.

Most community problems offer multiple issues or points of entry, so there is a need to choose the right one for your group. The most important issue criterion is this: *does it excite the group?* If there are unmistakable signs of interest, like enthusiasm and a willingness to work on the issue, go with it if it also meets most of these additional criteria:

1. *The issue is timely and urgent.* There is nothing so dull as an issue whose time has gone or has not yet come. One gauge of urgency is the level of conflict over the issue; the higher the conflict, the more timely the issue is among the various actors involved. Once it has become "an emotional issue" it is ripe for action.

2. *The issue is specific and limited.* That means it is present in the community and obvious in its impact on the people there. The issue should be visible, touchable, and identifiable in particular people, policies, and places where action can be staged.

3. *The issue is winnable.* You need to test the chances of succeeding with your action objective. Advocacy action is not a calling to martyrdom, self-defeat, or suicide for your social concerns group. You need to calculate the risks, what you're up against, and your strengths in order to decide the question. What should not be questionable is your intention to win the issue and your courage to pick a fight where you have a reasonable hope of attaining the objective. The outcome, of course, cannot be guaranteed. While one loss will not necessarily demoralize your group, no group lasts very long if it never fulfills any of its objectives. If your cause is just, your objective is attainable, and your heart is in it—*GO FOR IT!*

4. *The issue will pull some support.* The last test of an issue is whether or not it will be supported by significant

others in the community and in the congregation. Even highly controversial issues can usually gain support with time, patience, and persistence by the social concerns group. An issue that receives 100 percent immediate support may be already won. One that receives no other support may not yet be ready for action.

You may have noticed that the organizing and planning progression we have been using is one of *winnowing, narrowing down, and making abstractions concrete.* One reason for this process is to help you escape "rhetorical romanticism" about problems and to get down to practical local realities.

The other reason for simplicity and increasing specificity in analysis and planning is to save you from conflict with members of the congregation. They may well block activism and cause dissension if an ideological trip is laid on them by the social concerns group. Don't lecture, "raise their consciousness," or straighten out their theology and politics in order to get a theoretical concensus before you act. *You will never reach consensus, nor will you ever get any action on the problem.*

Moreover, you don't need a theoretical consensus. What you do need is a presentation of a real local problem of human need and suffering that is focused in an immediate, concrete, and winnable issue that the congregation can understand and see a way to act upon. Go after the heart of the congregation rather than its head. That's where the real human action is.

Assuming that the issue has made it over all of the above hurdles, you are ready to do the strategic planning to carry out the action on the issue and to win your objective.

Do Strategic Planning for Action

You are now working and planning to win the issue you have chosen as a focus in order to address the larger problem. Contingency plans and fallback strategies are not appropriate at this point because they show mental reservations about succeeding and even expectations of possible defeat. If such things prove necessary, they can be done later during evaluation when the outcome of the action is known. The first step in strategic planning is to determine your *action-objective.*

The Action-Objective Decision

An objective is a clear, simple definition of a target to be reached. *An action-objective is specific behavior designed in response to the issue. It states what change you are trying to make happen. It aims to change!* (For example, get the city housing authority to substantiate and prosecute building code violations in Claim-Jump Realty properties within ninety days.) While your larger goal is to solve the problem you are working on, the action-objective is one step on the way and contributes to that end. The crucial test of an action-objective is this: *Does it contribute to a solution of the problem by changing the cause of the problem in some way?* Here are some suggestions about deciding your action-objective:

1. *Frame an action-objective that fascinates the social concerns groups and is feasible.* If people are going to put themselves on the line, they must be interested in the action because it has value to them and has a reasonable chance of succeeding and aiding in the realization of the objective. In other words, there should be some benefits for the actors themselves as well as the people in the community whose just cause they are advocating. The actors deserve some gratification too.

2. *Decide the action-objective together as a social concerns group.* The discussion will enable the members of the group to buy into the action and form it in ways that are appropriate to the nature and resources of the group. Each member has individual self-interests, personal responsibilities, and limits to what he or she is willing to do. Those commitments should be surfaced and recognized while defining the action-objective. This will forestall "a nonevent"—an action where no one shows up or those who do are unwilling to carry out the plans.

3. *Identify and enlist allies who will also support the action-objective.* At this point the power chart of the community, made earlier in the research phase, can be a handy tool. Public policies and institutional practices are more amenable to several pressure groups who are acting in concert on the same issue. Other organizations and their leaders may be able to supplement your own limited resources by contributing resources such as people power, money, approval, twin actions, contacts with "people on the inside," and so forth. Help should be sought and welcomed when given.

4. *Aim the action-objective at one cause of the problem and be specific about the change you want to achieve.* You will know that you have specificity when you have prepared a short written statement to pass out to the media and people you have targeted for the action. It should say who you are, the issue you are addressing, why you are doing it, the changes you want made, and what your group plans to do next.

Operational Steps to Take

Once you have decided on the action-objective it becomes the heart of the body of action you will build around it so that it can rise up and walk. These body parts are the operational plans and preparations that will enable the participants to act knowingly and together as a group. The following operational steps will be helpful in attaining your objective:

1. *Create a responsibility flow chart.* Get organized for the big day by devising a time line, flow chart, or account-ability chart that diagrams this basic question about the operation: *Who will do what with whom by when?* Include all the members of the social concerns group in the chart and the specific tasks that have to be accomplished in order for the action to take place.

2. *Pray and fast.* In the midst of all this work and research about problems, issues, action-objectives, and as you gird yourself to face dragons and devils out there in the world, stop regularly. Stop for the ultimate and eternal perspective that will help keep you human and keep your sense of humor intact. It will also free you from either playing God or believing that all those Philistines are twelve feet tall. Bible study and prayer are the most radical activities that your social concerns group will ever undertake. They give ''shy persons the courage to get up and do what needs to be done,'' as Garrison Keillor says. (Refer again to the Bible study resources in Appendix F.)

9

Getting Down to Brass Tactics

To claim to be a Christian who loves God and neighbor and not to attempt to be an effective person in the formulation of just social policies is to talk nonsense in the modern world.[1]

You may begin to feel uncomfortable at the mere mention of doing something loud or brassy as a social concerns group of the local church. Do not be anxious for tomorrow. The tactical decisions are yours alone to make and you will not be asked to do anything that violates your nature and purpose as a group or your Christian conscience and ethical principles.

However, remember that there is *a profound difference between manners and morals,* and the two should never be confused. The Christian faith is concerned with what is right and just under God's sovereignty, while manners are ruled by mortals who would have considered Jesus' disciple band of working-class people to be social outcasts and cultural lepers. Jesus loved those disciples, bad manners and all, and you can count on the same for your discipleship.

Choosing, Defining, and Implementing Tactics

Choosing the tactic(s) to achieve your action-objective is one of the most important decisions your group will make.

A tactic is a move you make, something you do, a technique employed in order to accomplish your objective and effect the change you want. That means it is practical and pragmatic while also being appropriate to the issue and the situation. Tactics should not be polluted with extraneous motives and needs, whether for power trips, publicity, "getting somebody," raising support or funds, or action merely for the sake of doing something. The sole purpose is to win the change.

Tactics are only employed in order to motivate decision makers and institutions to make those changes in policies, procedures, or structures that will increase social justice and decrease human suffering or deprivation. If you know the problem-issue and the target well enough to move into action at all, you will also be able to assess the kind of tactics appropriate in terms of the amount of pressure required. "Tactical overkill" is a waste of time and effort, and "combat" is foolish if cooperation will achieve the same results. The various tactical approaches for use in strategic decision making are outlined below.

1. *Low-Key Tactics.* Some groups like to begin with a personal approach to the decision makers. You simply share your data with them, ask for changes you want made, and seek to negotiate how change can take place with your help. This is a private, collaborative technique and it may work if the decision makers also want to see reforms made, or don't want public disclosure of the facts, or fear alienating your constituency. Letter writing also belongs on this level.

2. *Public Witness Tactics.* One can bring more pressure to bear by going public and invoking external sanctions like displeased peer pressure, higher authorities, and investigative committees. Using the political process also belongs here in terms of public disclosure of information, citizen lobbying, petitioning, and election campaign work.

3. *Public Confrontation Tactics.* At this point one has

moved from cooperation and public appeals to strong opposition to using public demonstrative acts such as rallies, marches, picketing, street theater, lawsuits, selective patronage, fasting, prayer vigils, and proxy challenges to exert some "push power."

4. *High-Pressure Tactics*. The maximum amount of nonviolent pressure is exercised in techniques of persistent contact, sit-ins to shut down the system, strikes, boycotts, civil disobedience, and noncooperation. At this level one may be involved in breaking public laws and be subject to prosecution by the civil authorities.

More intense power plays cross an important line by abandoning political and social action in favor of direct, desperate actions of violence against persons and property. The revolutionary acts to overthrow or eliminate opposition through violence. This behavior is repulsive to Christian social activists in an open, democratic society on grounds of conscience, tactical pragmatism, and ethical principles. Violence breeds violence, whether it is done by citizens or by government, and represents the bankruptcy of the whole social and political fabric. Like lies, unfairness to opponents, and violations of human rights and dignity, such tactics are blatantly immoral in contemporary America and should be rejected out of hand by Christians.

While committed to nonviolent means, Christians can still show a lot of courage and creativity in dramatizing injustices and exerting pressure for social change. It has been done in the civil rights and peace movements, and it will be done again when the injustices of government and society become intolerable to the Christian conscience. The action of your social concerns group may be far more modest, but your cause and your convictions are as important to the health of your community as larger movements are for the welfare of the nation. In choosing your tactics, here are some guidelines to follow:[2]

1. *There will be group disagreements on tactics*. The appropriate tactics to use to reach your action-objective are likely to be a point of wide or strong disagreement in your group, and even more so in the congregation. The process of making the decision can bring you to a halt or even terminate your group unless it is handled with all the skills of conflict management. Know those skills and use them to build internal support. (See Chapter 11.)

2. *The tactics should be flexible*. You use what you have to do what you can to effect change, so your tactics will have to fit the capabilities of your group. In addition to that, the tactics must be able to change as the circumstances of group interaction with the target changes so that you can threaten to use them, postpone their use, use them, and repeat them if required.

3. *The tactics should cause a reaction*. The worst that can happen to you is that you are simply ignored as irrelevant and impotent. The selected people and institution will do that if at all possible. You will have to get their attention and do something that forces a response. As Saul Alinsky said, "The real action is in the enemy's reaction."[3] Effective tactics will make them show their true colors in relation to your cause. As Alinsky also said, "Power is not only what you have but what the enemy thinks you have."

4. *Good tactics beguile, persuade, or force the target persons/institution to enact, cooperate with, or at least allow change*. That is another way of saying that if the tactics work you will win your action-objective. At a minimum, the tactics must make some progress toward that goal and not be playacting.

5. *As to the old "ends and means" debate, the gospel had better justify both or neither is worth doing by the church*. It is usually true that the loftier the human ends, the meaner the means people will employ to achieve those ends which are used to cover a multitude of sins. Jesus' end was the kingdom of God, his means were suffering servanthood and giving up life itself. You can make that the most meaningful test in the end.

6. *Any tactic that has the triple virtues of surprise, humor, and righteous demand wrapped up in one action is a sure winner*. (The problem is how to stay angry while laughing at your opponents' looks of surprise.)

7. *Identify the culprit*. Some person(s) has/have to be given the high honor of personally symbolizing the institution, corporation, agency, or group that you are acting upon. Responsibility for injustices should have a name and face, and usually does show itself through a representative person who personalizes the issue.

8. *Accent your opponents' errors until you've won your action-objective, then praise them for their virtues since they will have both—just like you*.

The Action Itself

This section can be summed up in only two words—*DO IT!* Complete the tactical action you have been planning all this time. There will of course be doubts, second thoughts, and cold feet because that's natural, especially with confrontations and high-risk actions.

Everyone who has ever done something like you've

planned has had the same last minute feelings. Be of good courage—those feelings and thoughts will disappear once you move into action. They are soon replaced by an energy that some say is an experience of the Holy Spirit.

There are some guidelines for action suggested by those who have a lot of experience with it. Here are a few of them:

1. *Don't be co-opted by the opposition.* While some compromises may be required eventually to resolve the issue, do not compromise easily or immediately. The experience of either great hostility or great magnanimity from the other side may be an attempt to neutralize your group and its objective. Or, they may offer some compensation or favor. You will need to decide your response to half-loaf offers and attractive alternatives to the change you want made.

2. *Beware of their crisis managers whose job it is to get rid of you empty-handed but feeling good.* Refuse their coffee and doughnuts politely, and also refuse to deal with their vice-president for public relations, their psychiatrist, and their chaplain. Demand to see the highest authority in the organization, whose name you should know from the biography you have!

3. *Keep your issue and demands simple and to the point.* Don't argue. Keep stating what you want, why you want it, and when you want it. Then say it again. Also, ask for it in writing and signed.

4. *Keep your sense of humor, never get ugly, and pray constantly.* The first is a saving grace. If you fail to do the second, it is counterproductive, and the third is a needed affirmation that you are not in control, nor are you there alone.

5. *Know when the action is to end.* Make some person responsible for signaling the group when the action is to be terminated; this termination point should be agreed upon beforehand by the group.

6. *Go out and celebrate together.*

7. *Regroup to evaluate your progress and to prepare for the next action.* (See Appendices I and J for some tools for evaluating objectives.)

10
Leadership Roles for Empowerment

And he called to him his twelve disciples and gave them authority over unclean spirits, to cast them out, and to heal every disease and every infirmity (Matthew 10:1).
"He who is greatest among you shall be your servant; whoever exalts himself will be humbled, and whoever humbles himself will be exalted" (Matthew 23:11-12).

Who's in charge here?

That is one of the first questions to answer to understand the dynamics of any social group. One seeks to identify *who is responsible for exercising certain essential functions* for the group that endures, works well together, and accomplishes its goals. Groups come and go, quarrel and agree, do the job and fail, and the skill levels of their leaders make much of the difference in what happens.

This chapter will outline some of the learnings of management theory concerning group life and leadership roles, especially in terms of building support. The social action group of a local congregation will be primarily concerned with the issues it is addressing and the social problems it intends to act upon. That can be a heady and exciting adventure.

Sooner or later, however, the group will confront some of the human obstacles such as group dissension, some opposition within the larger congregation, and conflict with people and institutions in the community who are asked to change for the sake of greater justice. The group will have "to get its act together before taking its show on the road."

Question Some Tired Assumptions

Our culture circulates some folk sayings about leadership that are often appropriated by the church. They should be examined before they are taken for granted or given the authority of wisdom. Here are some common truisms that can be challenged by the experience and learnings of good group leaders.

Myth #1: *A group always has one leader who is formally elected or appointed, and that person runs the group.*

True, sometimes the group has a person skilled in leadership, is able to identify him or her, and then elects that person to office. More often leadership goes to the one who is most vocal or is simply willing to do the work entailed, especially in voluntary associations such as the church.

Effective leadership is a skill that can be learned from experience, training, or good resources. Leaders are made, not born. Also, groups can be informally led by other participants who influence the direction of the group "from the pews," so to speak. This involves more than one leader in the democratic process.

Myth #2: *Leaders have a charisma that is easily identified because it is particularly characteristic.*

This myth is a legacy of our political campaigns for electoral offices and what the media have done to the biblical word *charisma,* or "gift from God." Three rebuttals can be offered.

First, there is no single, best way to lead a small informal group, least of all according to *Robert's Rules of Order.* As the New Testament suggests, "there are varieties of gifts but the same Spirit" (1 Corinthians 12:4) who is the unelected leader of every church group. God often chooses very imperfect and improbable people to do great things for justice.

Second, if leadership qualities were so easily identifiable, the most redeemed, loving, and just people would lead our churches and our society instead of the wealthy, the clever, and the powerful in office (count the number of millionaires in the U.S. Senate). Leadership is always a risk for those who choose as well as for those chosen, and no one can predict the results. One can only look for a person committed to the purpose of the group who is sensitive to human needs, is willing to share leadership, and can deal with conflict and enable the group to make decisions and move into action.

Third, leadership is an interpersonal function more than an individual personality trait of the leader. What a leader says and does to help the group plan, organize, and act are the important things—not charm and popularity. The group needs someone who can act out a social role that involves special people management skills, not play a personal role where the self is represented to the group.

Myth #3: *Good leaders have strong minds, thick skins, and wear a kid glove over an iron fist.*

The description of leadership in this myth is a good characterization of a U.S. Army general, a corporate business tycoon, an authoritarian father, and several of the ancient gods. In time, his or her group will either plot a revolution or go AWOL.

All of us have a need to lead at times. At other times we want to be led by someone else. Whether or not we want to lead can change according to circumstances too numerous to name or even know. As social beings, we move back and forth in different group settings between relational poles like these:

control $\longleftrightarrow$ submission

independence $\longleftrightarrow$ dependence

compromise $\longleftrightarrow$ combat

autonomy $\longleftrightarrow$ authority

Where people are, what is going on in a particular group, and the style of leadership used are all factors in the group dynamic. The bewildering mix may result in a cooperative group or one divided in a conflict, an immobilized group or one with high energy for work.

The art of leadership is the skill to lead and also to be led, to balance individual needs and group goals, to meet member needs for support and also needs for control, and to help the group survive the conflicts and reach a cooperative working style. Leadership may be more art than science. One can take heart in the fact that, all things being equal, we humans are equally as capable of compromise and cooperation as we are prone to deadly and destructive behavior. Good or poor leadership can make a big difference in which way a group goes.

Consider Basic Leadership Functions

Organizational theory has done some work on the motivation of individual members who join organizations in order to meet their own personal needs. It is suggested that *people join organizations hoping to experience some meaning or excitement they have not found in the rest of their lives.*

One theorist proposes a typology of motivations and rewards received that is shown here in adapted form, reflecting our church language in some places.

One interesting thing about that secular list of motivations and rewards of group membership is how well the church can compete with other social organizations—if the church is alive, faithful to its nature and mission, and is socially concerned as a congregation. There are great multitudes of

Sources of Meaning in Organizations[1]

Opportunities Sought and Personal Values Received

Opportunity	Value/Need Met
1. A chance to test oneself as an independent person	Self-reliance and self-fulfillment
2. A chance to experience a social experiment	Human community and integration of life
3. A chance to do something well	Excellence and new accomplishments
4. A chance to do something good	Caring and service to others
5. A chance to change the way things are	Activism and social responsibility

people who, for a place in the sun and a little warm human community, will work to do some good things and engage in social action in order to change the way things are. The church can offer a source of meaning which makes it unique among all other social organizations—the gospel of Jesus Christ and God's kingdom coming in this society.

There are four basic leadership functions to be exercised in a group or a congregation, especially during times of controversy and conflict over social issues and actions.[2]

Function 1: Empower People to Act in the Most Mature and Responsible Ways Possible

Conflict can bring out the best or the worst in people, depending on how weak or powerful they feel in a given situation. People who feel that they are weak, in the minority, and are losing the struggle to achieve their objectives are more prone to use unfair, underhanded, and destructive tactics. Dirty fighting is a sign of powerlessness and desperation by subordinate and dependent people. It is sometimes rationalized, oddly enough, as a necessity in order to make it "a fair fight" among unequal opponents.

In that case, a leader can make two opposite but equally serious mistakes. He or she can overpower them. The leader asserts strong authority, puts them down, and weakens them further in order to strengthen his or her own leadership in the situation. That only aggravates the problems of powerless people.

Second, a leader can give in to them. This mistake involves using the powers of leadership to give them what they want, or work to accomplish their goals for them. That keeps them dependent and protected, while the leader then becomes powerless to do anything but continue meeting their needs. Once you stop meeting their needs, they will turn on you with blame or punishment.

The third alternative is for the leader to act in ways that

empower the powerless, enabling them to express their best selves and fair methods in striving to achieve their objectives. It is *the mentor role* that nurtures independence and self-reliance in people, not that of an authoritarian parent or an indulgent uncle. It is mature, independent people who are best able to represent themselves in conflict and to engage in interdependent problem solving and integrative compromises beyond "a victor-vanquished final battle."

Function 2: Nurture Trust in the Group and Its Leadership

The liberating leader is one who strengthens and encourages a group rather than dominating the group or trading services and favors for group loyalty. Such a leader nurtures trust in the group itself and in the leadership role, giving the group confidence in itself, its cause, and its chances of achieving its objectives. Trust enables people to communicate with each other directly and honestly, which is important for resolving conflict in its earliest stages, whereas distrust exacerbates conflict.

A good leader inspires a group and gives it heart through his or her own faith in what they are doing and in the abilities of the members. The leader must first be a true believer in the group purpose and communicate that faith as a buoyant confidence in the integrity and worth of the cause. Then the leader will articulate credible ways of achieving those ends. Finally, the empowering leader expresses his or her trust in the power of people to accomplish the tasks and the objective of the group.

People in any group will be at different stages in maturation that may range all the way from childlike dependence through adolescent rebellion to full independence enabling cooperation among equals and interdependent responsibility. A leader works with whoever is there and works with them wherever they are, enabling people to buy in where they can while continually urging them to grow into fully adult and collaborative responsibilities for the life of the group.

Function 3: Enable the Group to Define and Own Common Goals

Disowned or unclear goals are major sources of group conflict in the church, reflected in statements such as, "The church has no business becoming involved in the social, economic, or political problems of the community." Others would say just the opposite. Those who hold the abstention view would state that, "The real purpose of the church is to minister to the religious and spiritual needs of its members." Two conflicting church purposes are already on a potential collision course.

The goals and objectives of any organization are derived from its shared purpose for existing in the first place, or the needs it was established to meet. The needs are those of individual members and the organization as a whole, and sometimes the needs of the environment in which it is set. In the illustration just shown, the conflict is over whether or not the church exists to serve the needs of the community, and, if it does, which specific community needs are to be legitimately served.

There are many church resources designed to help your group define its purposes, goals, and needs.[3] Here we can only emphasize the importance of the leader's role in the process as a way of preventing or resolving conflicts. Some techniques that are used to help a defused group achieve a common vision are:

● Appealing to the emotions and values of group members.

● Articulating shared hopes, values, interests, and exciting possibilities.

● Identifying common strengths of the group members.

● Using communication styles that incorporate human and biblical imagery and express the enthusiasm of the leader.

● Being positive and emphasizing the great possibilities open to the group if it will work together.

Function 4: Enable the Group to Find Ways to Achieve Its Goals

A liberating leader will follow through by enabling the group to act on its goals in ways that give a good chance for success. Few things will demoralize a group as quickly as patently impossible goals, or exciting goals that are impossible for that particular group to achieve. In this case leadership involves empowerment because people are demoralized if they believe that they are helpless and nothing can be done, or that their actions will be futile.

All great populist leaders are people of great faith and courage who often happen to be good action strategists as well (for example, Mahatma Gandhi and Martin Luther King, Jr.). There are at least four ways that a leader can foster empowerment in a group ready to go to work.

1. *Create a sense of forward movement.* This is often begun through calculated group experiences that are positive because they are successful on an elementary level. The leader starts on limited and realistic action objectives which are well within the achievement capabilities of the group. The leader then moves "off the dime" in order to start building momentum and confidence.

2. *Maximize initiative and independence.* The empowering leader gives people as much self-control and responsibility as they are willing and able to handle, sharing the power. Since helping others often can ratify their weakness, the leader helps only when requested to do so, and then in ways that minimize dependence. In addition, the leader asks for help when he or she can use it in order to increase the

reciprocity between increasingly equal members of the group.

3. *Foster collaborative work styles.* Collaboration means working together and mutually sharing responsibilities for a task, or interdependence among strong individuals. This is the most effective kind of leadership because one joins the group in achieving its objectives, rather than either "doing it for them" or "abandoning them to their fate." Good leaders who have strong followers work themselves out of a job and become "first among equals."

4. *Give out praise, hugs, and honors.* Recognition or praise is one of the most important jobs of a leader, one to be indulged frequently and never delegated to others. In fact, if you don't enjoy doing it you should not be in a leadership position, even if you're elected to one. Rewards for desired behavior achieve far more than punishment of unwanted behavior because rewards are positive—they are good news—like the gospel itself. That is what we are all supposed to be about in the church, after all, where we celebrate good news overcoming the bad news of sin and death. Celebrate your people who do good things well.

11

Conflict Management in the Church

And there arose a sharp contention, so that they separated from each other; Barnabas took Mark with him . . . but Paul chose Silas and departed, being commended by the brethren to the grace of the Lord (Acts 15:39-40).

Conflict always involves people. However, it is not always fomented by the participants alone. They may be caught in a larger web of contradictions that deter peaceful and humane solutions to human problems. In the Bible, these contradictions are called "the principalities and powers" (Ephesians 6:12). In organizational theory, they are named "systemic factors" that influence the shape and style of conflict in organizations.

Quickly . . . state the rules that govern conflict in your local church and make it Christian conflict in contrast to the other kinds. If you cannot tick them off, is it because you don't have any rules, or because you won't know the ones you have until the day when church conflict erupts?

You may be trapped in church silence on the matter since only the Catholics and the Anglicans have published canon laws which define church doctrine and church order. All the rest of us Protestant Christians live by the Bible with a little tradition thrown in. Your local church folk traditions may surprise you when you happen to cross them innocently.

Some More Assumptions to Question

There are two myths that surround conflict in the church.

Myth #1: *Conflict will divide a church and cause it to lose money and members.*

This charge must be heard and met because it is the one most often leveled against those clergy and social concern groups who advocate that the congregation act on social justice problems in the community.

There are cases where individual church members have dropped out because the pastor or the parish became too involved in social issues. Everyone has heard a story like that, but anecdotal evidence does not represent credible statistical findings based on controlled methods of sociological research.

Some solid church research has been done in the last fifteen years that calls into question this popular myth. *The research supports these judicious conclusions:*[1]

1. There are various forms and degrees of social action, and some are neither controversial nor divisive. Lay people are not enthusiastic about radical social action, but they will generally support social concerns involving charity and evangelical missions.

2. Some forms of involvement in social issues have resulted in some laypersons withdrawing their support from local churches.

3. Surveys of clergy over the years, as well as research evidence, show that new people often join the church and members often increase their financial support because the church becomes involved in relevant social issues in the community. These positive gains are often disregarded even though they may equal or outnumber the stories of defections.

We all look for reality-confirming evidence for our hates and loves, our fears and fascinations. The research on church social involvement shows this encouraging fact for your social action group to celebrate: *Act for the kingdom of God in this society and some will leave you, more will join you, and you will have more unity of purpose!* Expect some defections. Remember what happened to Jesus' support the closer he came to the cross of suffering.

Myth #2: *Conflict is always bad because it is a sign of failure.*

Whether or not conflict is bad or is a sign of failure depends on the reasons for the conflict, its intensity and effects, and how the leader and the group deal with it. If it is allowed to weaken or destroy a group, it is bad; but when conflict is faced and handled in responsible ways it can also enliven and strengthen a group or local church.

For example, here are four reasons why controversy and conflict may sometimes be welcomed as a sign of growth, or even as an inspiration of the Holy Spirit in the life of the local church:

1. Conflict may be a healthy sign in churches where members relate to each other distantly and superficially, controlled by manners and niceties that keep everything polite and always agreeable. After all, a hard look at the biblical mandate of the church to risk its life for God's mission in the world is bound to be controversial.

2. Conflict may be a prerequisite of church growth in congregations that prize harmony and homogeneity so highly that people unlike themselves—from another race, social class or culture, for example—are subtly excluded from membership. Different people are feared and not tolerated, so they will definitely cause conflict if introduced at coffee hour after worship.

3. Some conflict, moderated by good leadership, is a controlled expression of the latent hostilities and aggressions of people and can be therapeutic for group life. Surfacing these feelings may "clear the air" and be a better alternative to having them displaced or built up to explosive levels.

4. Conflict can wake up a sleeping congregation and bring some excitement and challenge into an otherwise dull and apathetic community of people. One may conjecture that more local churches die of boredom than perish from controversy and conflict. Some stress stimulation is necessary for activity, striving, and learning in an individual or a social group. Then and now, Jesus came bringing a threat to some and peace to others.

Congregational Norms

Every human family, group, organization, and society has norms governing the behavior of members. These standards have two characteristics that are relevant for our discussion of church conflict.[2]

1. Norms are unwritten rules formed to control group functioning and to regulate the relationships between members. Being unwritten—and some would even say they're unconscious—they usually become explicit only when they're questioned or broken because everybody just assumes them.

2. Norms not only carry prescriptions for acceptable behavior but also carry penalties. The punishment may range all the way from verbal disapproval to expulsion from group membership.

There are several reasons why a congregation, when experiencing increasing conflict over the positions or actions of the clergy or the social concerns group, should get its norms for managing conflict "up on the bulletin board" for all to read.

1. Some churches have *norms that prohibit any real conflict at all*. Often based on shallow interpretations of biblical themes like "peace" and "love," conflict is feared and squelched because it is taken to be a sign of Christian failure. Or, in some cases church members simply stone

the prophets bearing a burning coal of truth. All those who cause trouble are immediately pressured to shut up and conform or get out because they are rocking the ark. It is a repressive norm.

2. Some churches have *norms that hinder rather than help the congregation deal with conflicts over social issues*. A typical rule of this kind says that all church conflicts are to be informally contained and privately settled outside of public meetings. Direct, open, and public questions and challenges are called "troublemaking agitation and disloyalty." It is a suppressive norm that allows only back room deals.

3. Some churches have *norms that support normal Christian conflict* and they have developed fair ground rules for conflict resolution. Such churches usually honor diversity, differences, and open confrontation where fair limits are set on ways of acting. Backbiting, rump groups, and secrecy are censured in this case. It is a healthy, open, and democratic norm.

Suppression and repression of church conflict only increase the debilitating stress and fear in the life of the congregation. Rather than solving the problem, such norms

usually make things worse by prolonging the turmoil, putting the conflict out of reach, immobilizing the members, increasing polarization, and setting the community up for a big battle one day that could split the church permanently. The shame of it is that it can be managed in ways that could strengthen the congregation rather than shatter it.

A better approach to handling conflict is an open and above-board process that surfaces the present conflict norms held by the congregation for all to see and understand, and enables the members to write new rules and penalties that the congregation as a whole will be able to support. Know the rules and, if you don't like them, change them. Then communicate them to everyone.

Some Guidelines for Conflict Management

Conflict management is a skill that can be learned since it is neither a mystery nor magic. Exercised as such in the life of the church, it can be one of the contemporary *charismata* given by the Spirit to be used for ''the upbuilding of the body of Christ,'' which is not to be divided or dismembered.

There are no guarantees that every conflict situation can be successfully managed to an equitable and healthy resolution. Circumstances can vary widely along with the insights, timing, and leadership of the people involved. The worst approach is to do nothing or to postpone intervention until the situation is desperate—with angry factions, dirty tactics, traumatized people, and members leaving the church.

Here are some guidelines for conflict management suggested by people who have experience and skill in the art form. These guidelines are addressed to those involved as participants in controversies as much as those who would serve as referees of a dispute.

1. *The goal is de-escalation and resolution in most cases*. You want to move beyond conflict by going through it in fair, limited ways that result in a definite conclusion—win, lose, or negotiated compromise—but most of all with the unity of the congregation intact.

2. *Control yourself at all times*. You cannot control the behavior of others but you can stay in charge of yourself. Model the fair, reasonable, and loving behavior you expect from the opposition. Don't get carried away by your position, your feelings, or your opponents.

3. *Objectively describe what is happening*. Do it for the sake of others as much as for your own understanding, and do it without accusation or blame. Most conflicts are confusing, the discussion goes in circles, and people talk past one another without listening to one another. Map out the terrain and the players. An agreement on what's going on is a constructive step for all involved.

4. *Invite participation in a mutually designed process to solve the problem*. Encourage a common plan to resolve the matter that is fair, orderly, and moves slowly through decision making on a time line. Postpone fighting for planning the process of conflict resolution, and have a plan to propose.

5. *Track the issue development along with how you are proceeding*. Clear issue definition is very important because ideas, assumptions, and convictions are in conflict as well as people who hold them. The issues can change during the process and new issues may be introduced. Identify such developments and their meaning in terms of changed positions.

6. *Agree on the boundaries of the conflict*. There are two kinds of helpful limits: one is the ground rules which will control behavior in the conflict, and the other is limiting contacts between the disputing parties through moratoriums and turf lines so that both may coexist in the same organization while the conflict is being settled. Give each one a space and put some space between them.

7. *Create a conflict-resolution process*. Who will do what where and when, and how will it be done? The process will name the actors in each stage of decision making, what information is to be shared, and who will make the final decision by what deadline.

8. *Emphasize the purposes and values shared by the participants*. This goes directly against the grain of conflict, and participants are often unwilling or unable to reaffirm their common interests before they get on with their combat. To admit that we have far more in common than in our separation removes the poison from the arrows. An outside party may have to point out the similarities for them.

9. *Describe, describe, describe . . . and lay off the attacks and threats*. State relevant things such as your motives, words, actions, and goals in order to positively portray your case. Stand on your record rather than negatively attacking the persons and positions of the opposition. Threats to exercise harmful power in retribution show a lack of confidence in the merits of your case which needs strong-arm tactics and suffering to prevail. Of course, you do have a right to deter aggression and to defend yourself if need be.

10. *Keep the parties talking and participating in the process*. Conflicts need the medicine of increased conversation and full disclosure where everything is put out on the table. You are after the truth. Walkouts prevent any progress. Larger groups will enable the presence of non-combatants and neutralists who can have a salutary effect.

11. *Redefine the problem, if possible, or state it in other ways*. Some definitions of the issue may increase the conflict with accusations, threats, or preemptory conclusions about the causes and the outcome. The problem should be defined as fairly, objectively, and dispassionately as possible.

12. *Try a negotiated settlement when neither side will win or give in*. A half a loaf may be all that is possible in some cases, and a negotiated settlement may augur better for the future unity of the organization. You can give away

minor issues and stand fast on the big ones if you are not frozen into a total package victory. Magnanimous gestures can be used to ask the other side to give some too.

13. *Seek third party intervention.* The possibility of introducing a higher authority or person skilled in conflict management should be considered at any point. A neutral outsider acts like a judge in adversary proceeding and can often cool things down, make sure that fair rules are kept, and elicit the best from the participants.

Constructive Conflict

Times of conflict will be normal in the local church where members are struggling with the Word of God over issues of Christian faith and obedience. It was so in the early Corinthian church, and in every church enlivened by the Spirit to work for the coming of God's kingdom in this world and this time.

Conflict means that something important to people is at stake. No one wastes energy over the trivial and the innocuous. If there is never any conflict over God's call to care for the life of the world and seek public justice, the congregation is either mightily redeemed or mighty dead.

Times of conflict can be normalized if the members will face the issues openly and honestly, commit themselves to a fair process for working it out in good faith, and hold fast to their first loyalty to the church and the gospel. On the other side of conflict there is an even stronger church and more vital faith which are gifts to those who have suffered conflict and worked it through to the point of resolution and reconciliation.

Concluding Words

To those of you who are members of social concerns committees or similar church groups: We sincerely hope that this book will provide you with affirmation, insight, and inspiration in your efforts to help your church reach out in caring love to its community.

To others of you who read this book and find yourselves on unfamiliar, uncharted ground: You may be just beginning to explore some new biblical understandings of love for your neighbor. You may have only recently begun to become aware of the concerns of the community around you. You may belong to a church that has yet to give significant consideration to ministry in its community. You may only now be awakening to your challenging responsibility and opportunity as a lay minister to impact the life of your community. You may be overwhelmed at the thought of confronting and seeking change in the community systems and structures that may hold persons as victims of injustice.

The Good News is that it is all right to be where you are in relation to your spiritual growth! God loves and cares for you where you are and calls you to continued growth in discipleship. As a follower of Christ you are a part of God's kingdom that is and is to come! You are a servant of God who with other believers prays, "Thy kingdom come, thy will be done on earth as it is in heaven." You are a member of the church, the body of Christ in the world!

You and others like you are not on this pilgrimage alone. Along with Christ's commission to "Go therefore and make disciples of all nations . . ." is the promise of his unfailing presence, "and lo, I am with you always, to the close of the age" (Matthew 28:19-20).

You can make the caring difference in your church and community. Go forth in Christ's name!

Appendix A

How to Get and Use U.S. Census Reports

U.S. Census Bureau information can be obtained from many locations. Local libraries often contain data in print form as published by the Census Bureau. Regional Planning Commissions may have additional and more detailed information beyond the census data. There are also twelve regional offices of the census Bureau that contain detailed information on the regions which they serve. The offices are listed at the end of this appendix. These agencies provide information at no cost and offer great service in using demographics.

State Data Centers set up by the Census Bureau and the states also offer services. In these cases some services may have fees for use, particularly if computer analysis of data tapes is required.

It is necessary to understand some census geography and to identify the boundaries of population areas in order to use demographics. For most community development planning, the area and demographics of the census tracts will be most useful. These tracts are defined by the Census Bureau and the information is printed on tract maps. Block groups and the block census areas are smaller than the tract areas. However, not all tracts are divided into blocks and block groups. Minor civil divisions, census divisions, places, counties, states, and other aggregated areas including metropolitan areas are larger than the tracts. The agencies mentioned are sources of information about the particular census geography for the areas of your interest.

Another source of demographic information is Census Access for Planning in the Church (CAPC). This organization, sponsored by many denominations and councils of churches, maintains a computerized file of census data. The data files are searched by the census geography and the census variables to produce a custom report for specific purposes. CAPC reports include long, medium, and short profiles for any area of 1980 data, as well as a 1970-1980 profile comparison of selected data for any area. These reports vary in cost depending upon the length of search, but are usually in the $40 to $90 range. The address of CAPC is Center for Social Research in the Church, Concordia College, 7400 Augusta Street, River Forest, IL 60305. The telephone number is (312) 771-8300, extension 299.

The use of computer data bases accessed on-line from computer terminals is growing and will become a more attractive source of census information. National Ministries, ABC/USA is a subscriber to a service of the Glimpse Corporation called Statistical Analysis and Retrieval System (STAR). This system provides custom reports of 1980 data for many census areas. The number of areas will be expanded, and 1985 estimates as well as 1990 projections are scheduled to be added to STAR. Reports can be quickly produced by National Ministries and mailed to anyone requesting information for a low cost. For further information about STAR reports, write or call American Baptist Churches in the U.S.A., National Ministries, Research and Development, P.O. Box 851, Valley Forge, PA 19482-0851. The telephone number is (215) 768-2411.

Information Services Specialists in Bureau Regional Offices

Information services specialists in each of the twelve regional offices of the Census Bureau answer questions about census publications and products and help users locate and use census data. They also conduct workshops and make presentations on census programs and services.

Atlanta, GA 30309: Room 625, 1365 Peachtree St., N.E., telephone (404) 881-2274

Boston, MA 02116: 10th Floor, 441 Stuart St., telephone (617) 223-0226

Charlotte, NC 28202: Suite 800, 230 South Tryon St., telephone (704) 371-6144

Chicago, IL 60604: Suite 1304, 55 East Jackson Blvd., telephone (312) 353-0980

Dallas, TX 75242: Room 3C54, 1100 Commerce St., telephone (214) 767-0625

Denver, CO 80226: P.O. Box 26750, 7655 West Mississippi Ave., telephone (303) 234-5825

Detroit, MI 48226: Federal Bldg. & U.S. Courthouse, Room 565, 231 West Lafayette St., telephone (313) 226-4675

Kansas City, KS 66101: One Gateway Center, 4th and State Sts., telephone (913) 236-3731

Los Angeles, CA 90049: Room 810, 11777 San Vicente Blvd., telephone (213) 209-6612

New York, NY 10278: Federal Office Bldg., Room 37-130, 26 Federal Plaza, telephone (212) 264-4730

Philadelphia, PA 19106: William J. Green Jr. Federal Bldg., Room 9244, 600 Arch St., telephone (215) 597-8313

Seattle, WA 98109: Lake Union Bldg., 1700 Westlake Ave., North, telephone (206) 442-7080

Appendix B
Interviewing Community Leaders

WHO AND WHAT TO ASK

Each community is different. The titles held by community leaders are different. The employment base is different. Community attitudes also differ from place to place. However, every community has persons in leadership positions. These leaders should know what is happening in and to the community. Interviewing such leaders is an important way of gathering information about a community.

The following pages describe fifty possible types of leaders. The various parts of community life are divided into categories, such as: education, government, business, and industry. *You do not need to interview every type of leader suggested in these pages, but you should try to see persons from each of the categories.*

Some questions should be included in every interview. Other questions will be "tailor-made" to a specific leader because of his/her responsibility. Additional help concerning interview techniques can be found in "Since You Must Ask" by Lawrence Janssen.*

Questions to Be Asked in Every Interview

- What is your name and position? (If not already known.)

- What do you feel are the most critical needs, problems, or issues in your community?

- What kind of response do you see the community making to each of these needs?

- What role do you feel churches of the community are taking?

- What image do you have of_____?
  (name your church)

- In what way(s) can your church be helpful to you in your responsibilities?

Questions Which Might Be Asked in Any Interview

- How long have you held your present position? (Such information helps you in asking other questions. For example, a person who came to a position six months ago is usually less able to describe detailed facts about what happened two years earlier.)

- What do you particularly like about this community? Or, what about this community makes you particularly glad to live/work here?

- What about this community do you wish could be changed?

*Order "Action Guide 16" from: National Ministries Literature, American Baptist Churches in the U.S.A., Valley Forge, PA 19481 (Price: 25¢ per copy plus postage.)

EDUCATION

1. *Principal of the nearest elementary school:* Unless many students are bused from distant neighborhoods, the elementary school usually reflects most clearly the characteristics of its neighborhood. The principal usually knows children personally and has a feeling for their home backgrounds. Some questions for the principal are:

   a. What is the current enrollment of your school?

   b. In the last five (or ten) years what has been the trend of this enrollment?

   c. What future enrollment do you project for this school and what factors will cause any changes?

   d. What has been your mobility rate (children moving from or to the school) in the last year? What factors have caused this rate?

   e. Which minorities are in the school? What is the proportion of the total enrollment for each? What is the trend of minority group enrollment?

   f. What impressions do you have about the family background of the children in this school? What percentage of the children have both parents employed? What percentage are from one-parent families? What percentage are in economic poverty (or, how many are on a government-supported lunch program)?

   g. How well does the community support its schools? What acceptance do tax levies or school bonds have in the community?

h. Do you provide special education classes? For what kinds of handicaps or special needs? How many are involved? Do you feel there are persons not being reached by special education opportunities?

i. Have you developed any particular educational innovations? What are they? How well do you feel they are working?

j. Do you offer a hot lunch program? Do the children have to go home for lunch? If they go home, how many have an adult at home?

k. What type of recreational program is offered through the schools? How are the school building and the playground used after school hours and in the summer?

l. Have there been budget cuts which affected staff, extra curricular program, field trips, music, art, athletics? What is your evaluation of the effect of these cuts on the children?

m. What are some of your personal concerns for the children of the community? For the schools? For the community?

2. *Principal of nearby junior high school:* You would likely ask many of the same questions as listed above. You could also ask about the programs in sex education, moral or religious values, athletics, ethnic or minority group identity and history.

3. *Principal of nearby high school:* Many of the questions described above remain helpful at the high school level. In addition you may want to ask about student government, interscholastic athletics, dropout rates, the proportion of seniors going on to further education, and impressions about what proportion of high school graduates leave the community.

You could also ask about educational offerings for students who are interested in vocational-technical goals and about how the school handles the variety of interests students bring to the school. For example, are gifted students provided accelerated courses? The principal should also have a feeling about work opportunities and recreational opportunities for teenagers. You may

also want to ask about impressions concerning drug abuse, alcohol consumption, smoking, and teenage pregnancies.

4. *Student leaders at nearby high school:* You might work out such an interview with the principal and meet with students during a lunch hour. What are the impressions of such leaders as the student body president or the high school newspaper editor about the school and the community? What are the critical issues as they see them? What changes in school policy are they seeking? Do they receive support or resistance from school officials when, as student leaders, they represent student opinion about issues?

5. *Superintendent of schools:* From this person should come an overview of the public school system and its needs, accomplishments, goals, frustrations, and opportunities. Broad information about enrollment trends, ethnic and minority enrollment, special education, and continuing and adult education should be available. Policies about use of school property for the recreational and cultural needs of the community (the community schools plan) need to be revealed. What plans does the system have for new school construction? Are major changes planned in school policies?

6. *Director of Continuing or Adult Education for high school or community college.* Ask about degree and non-degree programs offered; enrollment trends; availability of off-campus courses for interested groups.

7. *President, dean, or other leader at nearby college:* Enrollment trends and projections, background of student body, particular programs being offered, town-gown relationships, needs of students or faculty and administration, how the college can be a resource to the community, expansion plans for the campus are topics for some of the questions to be asked. Also find out what proportion of students live on-campus, in the community, or commute. (Commuting students normally find themselves less involved in campus-related activities.)

8. *College student leaders:* Presidents of the student body and the newspaper editor could be interviewed together about issues as listed above in #4. Community attitudes, work

opportunities, and openings for volunteer service should be explored.

GOVERNMENT

9. *City or county manager:* When your community has such a person, he/she has the responsibility of coordinating the administrative services offered by the governmental unit. Some questions for the manager are:

    a. What is the present population for your community (city, village, county)?

    b. What is the trend of population change and what is projected for the future? What primary factors contribute to this trend?

    c. How adequate are such community resources as water, electricity, sewage disposal, solid waste disposal, etc.?

    d. What are the primary forms of employment in your community? Are these changing?

    e. Are changes expected in the way land is used in your community?

    f. How healthy is your central business district (or downtown)? How adequate is off-street parking? What proportion of storefronts are vacant?

    g. What services in your community are most effective?

    h. What services for your community are least effective?

    i. What citizen groups are heard the most in your office? What are their concerns?

10. *Mayor:* Even in communities which have a city manager, the mayor can be a very influential individual. Mayors can be asked many or all of the same questions asked of city managers. In addition, inquire about the political climate. How much agreement or disagreement is there in the community about what its major needs are and how these should be met? Who (by name) are the major leaders and opinion makers of your community?

11. *City council member, selectperson, supervisor, commissioner:* Persons elected to public office either represent voters of a part of the community or represent "at-large" catego-

ries. (In either case they had to take their views and opinions to the voters.) Probe with such persons their views about government services, community life, and the "health" of the community.

12. *City or county planner:* Many of the questions asked of the city manager apply to the planner also. This person should have important information about population trends and projections, land use, zoning, where growth (if any) will occur, the nature of residential or commercial development, trends of the church's specific neighborhood, housing patterns and availability. The planner can be asked about ecological concerns for the total environment.

13. *Employment Service (government) official:* You will want to know about employment and unemployment in your community, the type of employment available, the proportion of women in the labor force, impressions about needs in day care, stability of local industries and businesses, economic and job projections, etc.

14. *Welfare case worker or official:* Welfare includes financial aid and other services. Financial aid includes federally subsidized programs (Aid to Families of Dependent Children, Aid to the Blind, Aid to the Disabled, Old Age Assistance) and local and state supported programs (general assistance). You should find out how many cases (and persons) are represented in each category, what the trends for each category are, and how close financial support comes to actual living costs. How many cases does each case worker have? What are the other services being provided? What proportion of the need does each service reach?

15. *Urban Renewal or Rural Development official:* Seek information about the physical changes which have been achieved and which are proposed. What has happened to persons and families who were displaced? Probe the moral implications of the means used and the goals (ends) being sought in renewal and development efforts.

16. *Housing authority official:* You will want to find out what kind of low-income housing there is and how much has been developed in your community. How long must eligible persons wait for such housing? How many

are on the waiting list? Has your community provided housing for low-income families? The elderly? Is there a community room in one or more of the housing projects? If so, what use is made of it? What community groups could offer programs in the housing project?

17. *County extension agent:* County agents are a key contact about agricultural trends, land use, services to children, youth, homemakers, and older adults. Programs in nutrition, 4-H, or FFA can be explored. The relationships among other people-serving agencies and the quality of their services are often clearly seen by the county agent.

18. *Parks and recreation official:* Speak with a person involved with planning for parks and open space, programming for recreational needs of all ages, and preparing the budget requests for these programs. Playgrounds, gymnasiums, swimming pools, cultural centers, community centers, and parks represent the kind of public space for recreation every community might desire. What does yours have? How adequate are these facilities? Who can use them? What age groups receive most attention? What age groups are left out of planning and programming?

19. *Environmental Resources official:* What are the environmental standards governing your community's quality for air, water, solid waste, noise, and population density? What kind of exceptions to these standards are being permitted in Environmental Impact Statements? In what ways are citizens of your community involved in creating these standards and in enforcing them?

20. *Transportation official:* What are the available services in public transportation? What are current plans for increasing such services? What alternatives to automotive transportation are under consideration? Has your community tried to develop new forms of mass transit? What happened as a result? What do you feel is the public attitude toward mass transit? How well does traffic flow in and around your community? What changes in traffic flow are expected? What highways will be developed?

21. *Law enforcement officer:* A police chief can reflect on the entire range of crime and legal violations to be found in the community. A juvenile officer can focus more specifically on the forms that delinquency or juvenile dependency takes in your community. Drug abuse, alcoholism, shoplifting; police-community relationships; and specific services, such as the Police Athletic League, should be explored.

22. *Local judge:* This person usually has a perspective on the overall crime picture, the backlog in the criminal justice system, and on drug abuse, vandalism, and shoplifting. The present forms of judicial process, overall law enforcement, effectiveness of various institutions to which offenders and dependents are sent, and the probation system are other important topics to explore.

23. *Planning commission member:* Seek from this person the amount of information available to him/her as a nonprofessional in planning and his/her attitudes or concerns which influence public planning policy.

24. *Human relations commission member:* Explore whether the commission is only a "complaint" board which takes actions to better racial relationships when pushed to do so. Or, is it a board which initiates programs in the community? You may want to find out if the commission puts all of its efforts into race relations or if it also probes issues of sex orientation and age-group differences.

BUSINESS AND INDUSTRY

25. *Chamber of commerce official:* Chamber executives are responsible for public relations, services to tourists, stimulation of local business, industrial and community development, etc. These persons should know about the business climate, including the proportion of shopping done locally as opposed to that done in a nearby major city. Many questions asked of other persons about community life are appropriate for chamber officials.

26. *Local realtor:* Ask about trends of the persons who are moving into and out of the community. Where is new development taking place or where can it be expected soon? What are the trends in land value and land use? What is happening in terms of single family dwellings and multi-family

dwellings? What impressions do you have about specific neighborhoods of our community? How much housing is available for low and middle-income families? What are the trends in tax rates?

27. *Local banker:* A banker can share retail business trends, housing trends, population trends, economic trends, and projections for future growth and development. Inquire about what is happening to the neighborhood of the church.

28. *Local retailer:* A person in business often has information about the neighborhood, the kind of people with whom he/she does business, changes in attitude of the public, as well as specific information about trends and projections for retail sales.

29. *Tourism related person:* An owner or manager of a resort, campground, motel, or other tourist-related attraction/business can provide you information about visitors to your community. Where are people coming from? How long do they stay? What other services in the community do they ask about?

30. *Industrial leader:* An official of your community's leading industry should be able to help you learn how stable the employment base has been and is going to be. You can find out about labor-management relations, community attitudes toward this industry, whether the industry encourages its executives to be involved in the community, the economic outlook for the community, the industry's approach to equal employment opportunities and to environmental concerns.

31. *Labor union official:* If your community has a union that has strong influence, see one of its officials. Ask the union official about wage scales, working conditions, labor-management relations, safety on the job, the union's influence on the community, and its employment projections for the next few years.

32. *Grange leader:* Ask such persons about local agricultural trends and concerns as well as what types of services are being provided through the Grange and other farmer-oriented agencies.

33. *Service station manager:* Inquire about the neighborhood and what kind of changes have taken place over the span of several years.

COMMUNICATIONS

34. *Newspaper editor:* How extensive is the paper's circulation and what is its editorial policy about local issues? What provision does the paper make to cover all ethnic groups in the community? What is the policy of the paper about religious news? Does the paper see itself as having a role in mobilizing citizen support for key local issues?

35. *Radio-TV executive:* What is the station's range of influence and its editorial policy for dealing with local issues? How is public service time now being used? What can churches do to use mass communications better? What is the executive's evaluation of the community?

36. *Cable television manager:* How accessible is a cable TV channel for community programming or for church programming? Ask similar questions to those asked of newspaper and radio-TV people.

SOCIAL SERVICE AGENCIES

37. *Council of Social Agencies executive:* This person should know about the range of social services in the community and have a good grasp of the needs. Inquire what studies have been done in the community by other agencies and whether reports from these studies are available. Secure, if possible, a listing of the social service agencies available in your community.

38. *Community Mental Health director:* Explore the case load for the mental health center and the waiting time between contact and actually receiving service. What age groups show up most in the patient population and what seems to be the focus of their illnesses or needs? How does the center relate to other community agencies? How strong is the preventive aspect of the center's program?

39. *Health official:* How adequate are hospital services (including emergency room treatment)? What is the ratio of doctors to the population served? What is being done in terms of preventative medicine and the use of paraprofessionals? What is the official's evaluation of your community's drug-abuse programs, halfway houses, or other special services?

40. *Family counselor:* Explore family relationship trends, family tensions, styles of family life, broken homes, adequacy of other services for family units and single adults.

41. *Community fund director:* United Fund or the community fund-raising effort usually involves many persons from the community. In larger communities it may also involve paid staff. Such persons often have information about the community, the effectiveness of various agencies and programs, and unmet needs.

42. *Child care staff:* These persons should know your community's need for child care programs, preschool programs, nursery school, extended care, etc. They can also share what is now being offered.

43. *Older adult staff:* Persons working in programs with senior citizens and the senior citizen leaders themselves can provide information about the needs and concerns of older adults in the community. Housing, nutrition, transportation, group facilities and programs, employment, and health care are some of the topics which need to be explored as each relates to older adults. Also explore the present and potential volunteer service opportunities for older adults of your community.

44. *Representative of nearby institutions:* Explore the role such institutions have in your community and how your community relates to these institutions. Included among these are: retirement homes, prisons, nursing homes, mental hospitals, state schools, YMCAs, YWCAs, halfway houses, children's homes, etc.

OTHER LEADERS

45. *Pastor of nearby church:* Discover what is happening in and through his/her church. Ask about such things as trends in membership and attendance. Many questions asked of persons in other positions can also be asked of pastors.

46. *Local council of churches executive:* A paid or volunteer executive for a cooperating organization of churches usually is able to share information about churches doing creative programming. Explore what forms cooperative ministry is taking and what might be done.

47. *Minority or ethnic group representative:* Persons and organizations representing minority groups can share valuable insights regarding their concerns and how they perceive community attitudes. Blacks, Hispanics, Native-Americans, Asian-Americans, or other ethnic groups should be considered, including such groups as Southern Christian Leadership Movement, Urban League, and the American Indian Movement.

48. *Conservation or ecology organization representative:* Ask about efforts being made to protect wildlife, to meet issues of land use and ecology, to improve the quality of life.

49. *Neighborhood homemaker:* A homemaker who lives near your church can share important opinions on community services, local issues, images about the churches and family life. The homemaker can give you another consumer's attitude toward schools, retail stores, social service agencies, and governmental services.

50. *Losing candidate for major public office:* In many cases, a losing candidate in a recent election can provide perspectives and insights regarding the community which would be hard to get from current officeholders.

Appendix C

Needs Assessment—Conducting a Survey

Some congregations may wish to conduct a survey of residents in their target area to discover issues relevant to their neighbors. Outlined below are some helpful questions and steps.

I. Getting Ready

A. What are you really trying to accomplish?
1. What is the real purpose of the survey?
2. Do you already know or suspect what you are going to find out?
B. Who else is interested in a survey of needs? Have any other organizations, such as the ministerial association, social service organization, or government agency, already undertaken a survey? Would others wish to participate in the assessment?
C. Who can help? You may be able to get the help of social welfare agency personnel, teachers, or college faculty in the preparation or collection of your data. Your study could become a project of a high school or college class.
D. What are the geographic limits of your survey?
E. Who are the people you want to ask?
F. How many do you need to interview to get a true picture? Can the information you need be obtained through the study of recorded data or by observing conditions around you? Are there key leaders who possess the information you need, or do you wish to determine the problems needing most attention which are recognized by the general citizenry of your geographic area? Who you interview is more important than the number of people you interview. Ask yourself if all areas of the community are involved. Are we interviewing people from different segments of the community? Do we need to maintain a balance of men and women?
G. Will the survey be conducted door-to-door, through the mail, or by telephone?

II. Preparing for the Survey

A. What questions should be asked, and how should they be worded? Ask no more and no fewer questions than are necessary to provide you with the information you need. When you want to know concerns in general, include an open-ended question such as, ''What are your major concerns about your community/neighborhood?'' If a specific subject is of special interest you might ask, ''How do you feel about the adequacy (or ''supply'' or ''condition'') of (housing or whatever) in your community?'' Responses to open-ended questions are more difficult to tabulate and organize. They may cover many fields and range from the general to the specific.
1. You may wish to use questions that direct the response. ''Do you strongly agree; agree; disagree; or strongly disagree with the following statements?'' Or, ''On a five point scale—with 1 being the best and 5 the worst—please rate the following . . . .''
2. You may wish to include both open-ended and directed questions on your survey. Test out your questions on others before you finalize the survey document. You may be able to improve upon the way questions are worded and check for areas omitted through this step.
B. What do you want your respondents to learn? While your primary purpose is to gather information, the very act of explaining who you are, why your group is conducting the survey, and what you plan to do with the information may start people thinking about things in their community.
C. How should the survey takers be trained? The training of volunteers will vary according to the type of survey format selected. If the questionnaire is to be dropped off at homes and then picked up later, the instructions may include items such as these:
1. Which homes are to be visited (every other household or every fifth household)?
2. What does the surveyor say about the survey when leaving the forms? (For example, what group the surveyor represents, what the surveyor plans to do with the information, the surveyor's interest in knowing what people think, and assurance that the responses will be treated confidentially.)
3. How much time should the surveyor give people to complete the form? (Make sure that it is not more than a week).
4. Make a recommendation that the respondents be asked, when the forms are picked up, whether there were any questions. If they haven't completed the form, ask if they could fill it out then.

If a personal interview is planned, the helpers should assemble as a group and a trial run should be practiced in pairs. The discussion will help to clarify questions as to how to conduct the interview. Minor modifications in the form may then be made if necessary, and the data from the trial session can be tabulated to see if meaningful categories emerge from the responses. Meet to debrief after the survey has been conducted. Celebrate with your helpers.

D. Would a preliminary publicity campaign help? If people know a survey is coming, they are more likely to cooperate. Depending on the scope of the survey, you may wish to have announcements placed in bulletins of other churches in the neighborhood, at shopping centers, and through local news media to inform the residents of your purpose and survey dates.

III. Examining and Reporting the Results

If you have gathered large quantities of data from community citizens, you will need to classify and count your responses. Categories for similar responses to open-ended questions will need to be developed. Be sure to keep track of "no response" items as well as responses in each category, indicating whether it was a directed or open question. You will need to decide whether you wish to make a narrative observation about the data in your report or simply provide the data in tabular form and let readers draw their own conclusions.

Additional Related Resources

1. Gibson, Duane, ed., *A Citizen's Guide to Community Development*. Princeton: A Peterson's Guides Publication for N.U.E.A., 1981. The above outline was adapted from this pamphlet. The full text can be purchased from National University Extension Association, P.O. Box 2123, Princeton, NJ 08540

2. Gallup, George, Jr., and Davies, John, O., III *What My People Think: Gallup Survey Manual*. Princeton: American Institute of Public Opinion, 1971. This manual, designed for use in local churches, guides the reader through each step of public opinion polling and includes a sample questionnaire.

Appendix D
Church Participation Profile

In order to understand your church's relationship to your selected target community, you may wish to collect the data suggested below. The responses will indicate membership involvements in organizations and your greater sphere of influence. Some of the data will permit you to compare your congregation with your census profile of the community.

Church Participation Profile

To get a representative picture of your normal worshiping congregation, Church Participation Cards should be used on three successive Sundays in your main worship service. If you have more than one worship service on Sunday morning, they should be used in all services and the results combined. If your main service is at some other time, the cards are to be used then.*

NOTE: Each person is to fill out only one card during the survey. Cards should not be signed. To include all persons in the building during the worship period, use the cards in the nursery, extended session, Junior Church, etc. At least age and sex should be recorded for children in other activities held during your worship hour. Mark these cards to show where the persons were at the time, so that they are not confused with the worshiping group. If it is practical, include other information on the card for such children, though this might be difficult to do. Adults involved in special sessions during the worship hour should fill out a card completely.

In tabulating the cards, the result for those in the worship service should be kept separate from those in other sessions. (For example, there might be nine children from 10 to 14 in the worship service, and thirteen in this age group in the extended session.)

Below are the suggested steps for using the cards:

1. Select three successive Sundays when the congregation will be fairly normal. Avoid Sundays of unusually large attendance, such as Easter, and just before

NOTE: A count should be made of the number of persons in attendance and the number of cards turned in at each service in which the cards are used.

*Cards equal to 1 ½ times the average attendance will be needed.

**Many churches have expressed concern about the use of these cards in the worship service since it tends to break the continuity of worship. Each church will have to decide for itself the best time to use them. However, there is no substitute for securing this information from the persons who actually attend the worship experience. Using the cards early in the service or at the close may be less of a break in the order of worship. Care should be taken to use the cards when most persons will be present.

Christmas. Also, try to avoid Sundays of expected low attendance, such as summer or holiday weekends.

2. Distribute cards at a given point in the service** to all worshipers on the first Sunday; to those who have not previously filled out a card on the next two Sundays. *DO NOT* hand out cards with your worship bulletins. Make sure enough pencils are handy. Have people date their cards. Collect cards as soon as they are filled out.

3. The Pastor or a Planning Task Force member should explain the importance of the information to be given and should urge everyone to participate. Have cards filled out while the Pastor or Planning Task Force member stands before the congregation and reads the instructions given on pages 67 and 69. This will take a little time, perhaps 7 or 8 minutes, but there are no shortcuts to securing this information, and it will be valuable in making your analysis of the congregation.

4. Tabulate the results; record the total for all categories on pages 70-72. To tabulate, proceed as follows:

   a. Divide all cards into age groups found under item 6 on the card.

   b. Either use a blank card or make up a tabulation sheet for *each age group*, and proceed to tabulate cards BY AGE GROUP. When this tabulation is complete, there will be 14 separate sets of results.

   c. Add the totals in each category, and summarize them on the pages provided—pages 70-72.

Script for Leader when Using Church Participation Card

1. Check if you are a member of this church, a regularly participating nonmember, or a visitor. Visitors, please check also if this is your first time here.

2. Check the distance you lived from the building when you first began to participate. Normally this should be the most direct route. Estimate if you must.

3. In the same way, check the distance you now live from this building. Items 4, 5, and 6 are very important for a successful study. Please complete these questions since cards are not to be signed. Check in front of your appropriate sex, ethnic group, and age categories.

SAMPLE CARD

CHURCH PARTICIPATION CARD

Each person fills out only ONE CARD during the participation survey. Complete questions 1-6 for children under the age of 5. Members complete questions 1-15, others complete questions 1-13.

Date _____

1. **Which one are you?**
   - _____ Member
   - _____ Participating Non-member
   - _____ Visitor (_____ first time?)

2. **Where did you live when you began to participate?**
   - _____ Within 1 mile
   - _____ 1 to 2 miles
   - _____ 2 to 3 miles
   - _____ Beyond 3 miles

3. **Where do you now live?**
   - _____ Within 1 mile
   - _____ 1 to 2 miles
   - _____ 2 to 3 miles
   - _____ Beyond 3 miles

4. **Sex:** _____ Male _____ Female

5. **Ethnic Group:**
   - _____ White _____ Black
   - _____ Hispanic _____ Indian
   - _____ Asian _____ Other

6. **Age:**
   - _____ 4 or less _____ 5-9 _____ 10-14
   - _____ 15-19 _____ 20-24 _____ 25-29
   - _____ 30-34 _____ 35-39 _____ 40-44
   - _____ 45-49 _____ 50-54 _____ 55-59
   - _____ 60-64 _____ 65 or more

7. **Marital status:**
   - _____ Single _____ Married
   - _____ Divorced _____ Widowed
   - _____ Separated

8. **How long at present address?**
   - _____ Less than 1 year
   - _____ 1-2 years
   - _____ 2-3 years
   - _____ 3-5 years
   - _____ Longer (_____ years)

9. **Occupation and Employment:**
   - _____ Homemaker _____ Student
   - _____ Retired _____ Unemployed
   - _____ Employed

   If now employed, in what category?
   - _____ Professional, technical
   - _____ Farmer or farm manager
   - _____ Manager, proprietor, executive
   - _____ Clerical, office, etc.
   - _____ Sales worker
   - _____ Craft worker, production supervisor
   - _____ Operative
   - _____ Household worker
   - _____ Service worker
   - _____ Farm laborer
   - _____ Laborer
   - _____ Other

10. **Your present church responsibilities:**
    - _____ Church officer or board member
    - _____ Church committee
    - _____ Church school staff
    - _____ Choir member or usher
    - _____ Officer of church organization
    - _____ Other

11. **Church organizations to which you belong:**
    - _____ Children's _____ Youth
    - _____ Women's _____ Men's
    - _____ Mixed _____ Other

12. **Organizations to which you belong or in which you serve in the community:**
    - _____ Lodge or auxiliary
    - _____ Labor union
    - _____ Farm organization
    - _____ Professional organization
    - _____ Service club
    - _____ Scouts, YM, YW, 4-H, etc.
    - _____ P.T.A. or school group
    - _____ Veterans
    - _____ Civic boards, committees, etc.
    - _____ Other

13. **How many persons now live in your household?** _____

14. **Your length of membership here:**
    - _____ Less than 1 year
    - _____ 1 to 3 years
    - _____ 3 to 5 years
    - _____ 5 to 10 years
    - _____ Over 10 years

15. **Your method of joining this congregation:**
    - _____ Confirmation
    - _____ Baptism
    - _____ Letter
    - _____ Other

Rev. 9/76

Printed in U.S.A.

NOTE: Do not continue to answer for children under the age of five.

7. Please check present marital status:

   Single, if never married.

   Married, if now married.

   Widowed, if husband or wife is dead.

   Divorced, if divorced.

   Separated, if separated.

8. Check how long you have lived where you now live.

9. *Check only one occupation*. If you work at two jobs, check only the one which you consider your main job. If you are a homemaker or a student and are also employed, check which one you consider to be your main occupation. If you are not employed, check whether you are a homemaker, student, retired, or unemployed. If you are employed, check that *and also* the appropriate occupation:

   Professional includes teachers, editors, dentists, clergy, professors, instructors, doctors, lawyers, nurses, architects, librarians, social workers, engineers, etc.

   Farmer or farm manager—self-explanatory.

   Manager (other than farm), proprietor, and executive includes public officials, agents, buyers, officers, floor managers, personnel or credit officers, owners of private business, etc.

   Clerical and office worker—self explanatory.

   Sales worker includes workers in stores, as well as sales persons on the road.

   Craft worker, production supervisor includes skilled or semi-skilled workers engaged in production, as well as metal workers, etc.

   Operative refers to machine operators in which long apprenticeship is not required, and also truck drivers.

   Household worker refers to those employed in household services.

   Service worker includes firefighters, police, barbers, beauticians, janitors, porters, servants, waiters, ushers, soldiers, sailors, coast guard, practical nurses, etc.

   Farm laborer—self-explanatory.

   Laborer includes garage laborers, car washers, stevedores, gardeners, unskilled helpers in construction, manufacturing, etc.

   Other: Check here if you are not sure where you fit, and be sure to indicate your type of work.

10. Check all of your present responsibilities, adapting where necessary to the terminology you use (commission, department, instead of board, for example).

11. These categories are self-explanatory: Note: If Scouts, etc., are sponsored by the church, a check should be placed here by children and youth participating in the church-sponsored unit. If they belong to a unit not sponsored by this church, check under item 12.

12. These organizations in the community are self-explanatory. If an organization to which you belong does not fit any category, list it by actual name.

13. State the number of persons now living in your household unit.

14. Check the category for the number of years you have been a member of this congregation. Estimate, if necessary.

15. Check the method by which you joined this congregation: confirmation, baptism, transfer of letter, or other.

TABULATION SUMMARY SHEET
FOR CHURCH PARTICIPATION CARDS
(3 Sundays)

This is the summary sheet. Combine totals here from age-group tabulation sheets. Record the totals for all groups on this and the following page. Include adults in nursery or extended sessions with the regular participants. Make a special note of children included in special sessions.

                                    \# Cards   First Sunday _____
                                              Second Sunday _____
                                              Third Sunday _____

                                                    Total   _____
                                                                  _____

1. Which one are you?   \#   %
   Member .... _____ _____
   Participating Nonmember .... _____ _____
   Visitor (____first time) .... _____ _____

2. Where did you live when you began
   to participate?
   Within 1 mile .... _____ _____
   1 to 2 miles .... _____ _____
   2 to 3 miles .... _____ _____
   Beyond 3 miles .... _____ _____

3. Where do you now live?
   Within 1 mile .... _____ _____
   1 to 2 miles .... _____ _____
   2 to 3 miles .... _____ _____
   Beyond 3 miles .... _____ _____

4. Sex:
   Male .... _____ _____
   Female .... _____ _____

5. Ethnic Group:
   White .... _____ _____
   Black .... _____ _____
   Hispanic .... _____ _____
   Indian .... _____ _____
   Asian .... _____ _____
   Other .... _____ _____

6. Age:
   4 or less .... _____ _____
   5-9 .... _____ _____
   10-14 .... _____ _____
   15-19 .... _____ _____
   20-24 .... _____ _____
   25-29 .... _____ _____
   30-34 .... _____ _____
   35-39 .... _____ _____
   40-44 .... _____ _____

	#	%
45-49	___	___
50-54	___	___
55-59	___	___
60-64	___	___
65 or more	___	___

7. Marital status:

	#	%
Single	___	___
Married	___	___
Divorced	___	___
Widowed	___	___
Separated	___	___

8. How long at present address?

	#	%
Less than 1 year	___	___
1-2 years	___	___
2-3 years	___	___
3-5 years	___	___
Longer (___ years)	___	___

9. Occupation and Employment:

	#	%
Homemaker	___	___
Student	___	___
Retired	___	___
Unemployed	___	___
Employed	___	___

If now employed, in what category?	Male	Female	Total	%
Professional, technical	___	___	___	___
Farmer or farm manager	___	___	___	___
Manager, proprietor, executive	___	___	___	___
Clerical, office, etc.	___	___	___	___
Sales worker	___	___	___	___
Craft worker, production supervisor	___	___	___	___
Operative	___	___	___	___
Household worker	___	___	___	___
Service worker	___	___	___	___
Farm laborer	___	___	___	___
Laborer	___	___	___	___
Other	___	___	___	___

10. Your present church responsibilities:

	#	%
Church officer or board member	___	___
Church committee	___	___
Church school staff	___	___
Choir member or usher	___	___
Officer of church organization	___	___
Other	___	___

11. Church organizations to which you belong:

	#	%
Children's	___	___
Youth	___	___
Women's	___	___
Men's	___	___
Mixed	___	___
Other	___	___

12. Organizations to which you belong   #   %
    or in which you serve in the community:

    Lodge or auxiliary .... _____ _____

    Labor union .... _____ _____

    Farm organization .... _____ _____

    Professional organization .... _____ _____

    Service club .... _____ _____

    Scouts, YM, YW, 4-H, etc. .... _____ _____

    P.T.A. or school group .... _____ _____

    Veterans .... _____ _____

    Civic boards, committees, etc. .... _____ _____

    Other .... _____ _____

13. How many persons now live in your household?

    One .... _____ _____

    Two .... _____ _____

    Three .... _____ _____

    Four .... _____ _____

    Five .... _____ _____

    Six .... _____ _____

    Seven .... _____ _____

    Eight or more .... _____ _____

14. Your length of membership here:

    Less than 1 year .... _____ _____

    1 to 3 years .... _____ _____

    3 to 5 years .... _____ _____

    5 to 10 years .... _____ _____

    Over 10 years .... _____ _____

15. Your method of joining this congregation:

    Confirmation .... _____ _____

    Baptism .... _____ _____

    Letter .... _____ _____

    Other .... _____ _____

Appendix E
MAPS

Some maps will be helpful in your planning. Maps without colors are preferred. You can secure maps from your county office or city hall.

NOTE:

If maps are expensive or hard to obtain, you might put all your information on a single map. (This approach is not recommended since the result is hard to read.) A map with a scale of 800 feet to the inch is good for a city or metropolitan area. A smaller city might use a larger scale, and a larger city might have to use a smaller scale. For a town and country situation, a map with a scale not smaller than two inches to a mile should prove satisfactory.

1. Family or Household Membership Map

This map should be a clear map, preferably in black and white.

a. Locate the church building, and draw circles with 1-mile, 2-mile, and 3-mile radii, using the church building as the center.

b. Locate all households related to the church, using the following key:

Active household—blue dot.

Inactive household—red dot.

Regular participants but not members—green dot.

(This will include children in church school, or persons in other programs, where no family member is a church member.)

To make your map more transportable, use colored pencils or felt-tip pens rather than map pins for making dots.

Definition of a Household or Family: For this map include any family or household where at least one member is related to the church. In some cases two households or families will be housed in the same dwelling unit. In this case, two dots should be used. A widowed person or a single adult should be considered a separate household.

An Active Family is one in which at least half the family members who are also church members are active. *An Inactive Family* is one in which less than half the family members who are also church members are active. That is, if a husband and wife and teenage son are members of the church, and the husband never attends but the wife and son do, the family should be considered active. There is no universal definition for an active member. Perhaps this planning effort will stimulate the church to make such a definition.

Especially in Town and Country areas the map scale might be large enough to permit using a dot for each person in the household. Thus a given location might have blue dots for active members, red dots for inactive members, and green dots for those family members who are not church members but who participate.

As dots are put on, make a circle around each one representing a household in which there is a major church leader—deacon, deaconess, trustee, other board member, officer, choir director, etc.

2. Evangelism Map

This map should also be a clear map, preferably in black and white. Mark the church location as before, and make circles with one-, two-, and three-mile radii from the church building.

Locate on this map the residence of all persons who have joined your church during the recent past. Five years should be used, if possible, but the past three years will be sufficient if this is more practical. Designate new members as follows:

Blue: For persons in households already related to the church through membership.

Red: For young people whose families are not related to the church through membership.

Green: For adults with no previous household or family relationship to the church through membership.

Use one dot for each person.

3. Church Location and Community Factors Map

This map should also be a clear map, preferably

in black and white.

On this map locate churches of all faiths, including Jewish, Buddhist, etc.

In a city of more than 10,000 population, locate churches within two miles of the church building.

In a town and country area, locate all churches in the area covered by the map.

In any case, locate all churches of your denomination in the area covered by the map. Use a square and a numbered key (⬜) to designate churches.

Also show the following factors:

Blue: Rivers and water areas, including swamps.

Red: Traffic arteries, bus routes, etc.

Green: Parks, golf courses, cemeteries, or other large open spaces, such as the lawn of an institution.

Brown: Business areas.

Yellow: Industrial areas.

Black: Railroads.

You may wish to indicate the location of social welfare/service agencies in your target area or other key organization of influence/service.

Appendix F
Intermission: Biblical Reflections

After a rigorous exploration of the community, your head may be swimming with all the data collected and your feelings may be mixed about what you have discovered out there in the world. The impulse to withdraw, even "run away from it all," is a very natural reaction and should be accepted.

Christians have experienced something similar throughout the centuries. What is a church retreat, after all, except a time of withdrawal from the ordinary world for the sake of prayer and reflection on one's life from a biblical perspective? "Retreating" can be good for both the mind and the soul, to say nothing of its help in regrouping and energizing your social concerns group.

Karl Barth, the great Swiss theologian, once quipped that "the Christian should live with the Bible in one hand and the newspaper in the other." That describes your retreat task very well—to reflect on what you have learned about the community in the light of some biblical passages that may speak to your experience. For your retreat choose the Bible passages with a purpose in mind.

Here are a few suggestions about how your social concerns group might place itself in the way of the Bible as it speaks some loud and clear words of liberation and empowerment for Christians who are sometimes intimidated by the world. Work as a group with the passages in a series of Bible studies. You may choose to begin your group meetings with the study when you are processing your discoveries about the community.

The texts for your Bible studies are the following:

1. Liberty: Luke 4:16-30
2. God's Cause: Exodus 1:8-14; 2:23-25; 3:7-10
3. Knowing God: Jeremiah 22:13-16
4. True Worship: Isaiah 58:6-7
5. The Nations Judged: Matthew 25:31-46

With each passage, *pose three questions* that may help you unpack the text and your own experiences in the community:

1. *The Critical Question.* Who was the original speaker of this text and who were the persons to whom it was addressed? What was their world like at the time and how did the text serve to liberate and empower them?

2. *The Personal Question.* How does this text speak to me today as a Christian who is "making it" in this society and its economy? Think in terms of who you are—your job, income, social class, race, home value and location, education, friends, and so forth. What does it say to "social insiders" like me?

3. *The Social Question.* What does this text say to "social outsiders" today about our society's economy and politics? What would you be likely to hear if you were on the bottom of the heap? If you were a minority person? If you were unemployed and on food stamps? If you were old and you couldn't pay the taxes on your home?

You will be listening to each text from three very different locations knowing that the Word of God is always particular and concrete, saying different things to different people in various times and places. That is why words of liberation to the oppressed are also judgments on their oppressors, since God's speech is vital to all that all may live and justice may be done in the land.

Remember, God's Word is always a saving and liberating word to all of us. Whether it comes as judgment or grace, as promise or as pitfall, depends on who and where we are at the time and in which society. What is eternal and will never change is God's promise to be and remain sovereign and faithful to God's purpose of justice and genuine humanity for this world of ours, which includes you and your local community.

Appendix G
Congregational Inventory of Gifts

Exercise A: Personal Gifts Inventory

This exercise[1] will enable each member-minister in the congregation to identify what he or she has accomplished and what skills he or she used in doing those things. The inventory can be duplicated and inserted in the Sunday church bulletin as a method of distribution. It could look like this or be modified according to your insights and needs:

Directions: We want to know and to celebrate the things you've done which you have valued and enjoyed. Begin listing *what you value,* not what you think others would value. List past as well as current accomplishments and don't miss things that may now seem simple and unimportant. Follow the following steps in order to discover accomplishments of the past and talents for the future!

Step 1: On a separate sheet of paper, list the things you've done that you enjoyed and valued, no matter how minor or unimportant they may seem to others. List ten to twenty of them.

Step 2: Choose the five *accomplishments* which you value the most:

1.

2.

3.

4.

5.

Step 3: Starting with the first accomplishment listed in Step 2, recall what you did step by step to bring it off. Then put a mark beside each item on the gift/skills list below that was a talent used in the accomplishment. Add other skills if they're not on the list. Do the same thing with the other four accomplishments above.

Gifts/Skills

- Conceptualize, interpret
- Coordinate, organize
- Analyze, diagnose
- Research, investigate
- Compile, classify

- Compute, estimate
- Audit, do bookkeeping
- Copy, record
- Compare, observe
- Accept, advise, counsel, guide
- Negotiate, arbitrate, reconcile
- Instruct, teach, learn
- Supervise, manage
- Motivate, lead, inspire
- Perform, demonstrate
- Facilitate, moderate
- Persuade, sell
- Communicate, talk, write
- Serve, wait on others
- Listen, support, encourage
- Design, envision, create, invent
- Do precision work
- Construct, repair
- Do an artistic presentation
- Evaluate, inspect
- Inventory, catalogue
- Operate, drive, use tools
- Maintain, do caretaking
- Collect, arrange, display

  Other gifts/skills:

-
-
-
-
-

Step 4: Review each accomplishment and the skills used. For each one, select the two talents used that were most important for achieving it. Put two additional marks by the most crucial one and one additional mark by the other one.

Step 5: Add up the total number of marks by each talent on the list. Enter the talent used most frequently in Box 1 below, the second most used in Box 2, and so forth, until the pyramid of gifts used in your accomplishments is completed.

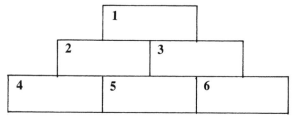

My Pyramid of Gifts

Step 6: See how talented you are! The last step is to sum up *your five principal personality traits* based on your talents and how you have used them. For example: patience, courage to risk, concern for others, following skills, leadership skills, friendliness, flexibility, optimism, practicality, theoretical skills, and so forth.

My Personal Traits

1.

2.

3.

4.

5.

Exercise B: Lay Ministries Inventory

This exercise[2] offers a tool that will enable the congregation to identify the things member-ministers are doing in the community beyond stated programs sponsored by the local church. These ministries are usually unclaimed and uncelebrated by the church. That's probably part of our blindness to the ministry of the laity.

The task is to survey the member-ministers on their community involvements. This can be done with a distributed questionnaire, personal interviews, or in group meetings. The important thing is to ask the right questions that will surface the community service actions performed outside the local church program. Questions like this could be asked:

1. Besides the church, to what other groups, organizations, and institutions in the community do you belong? What is the purpose/program of each one?

2. What is your role in each one? Do you have leadership responsibilities in any of these groups, organizations, or institutions?

3. Beyond your membership, do you volunteer your time/work anywhere? Do you give any personal services to persons or groups outside the church?

4. List the groups and causes *other than the church* to which you make charitable contributions. (List them in the *order of* the amounts given in the last year, but do not list the dollar amounts.)

5. Are there any ways in which you carry out your occupation that you consider to be part of your Christian ministry as a layperson? Identify them.

Appendix H
Resources for Planning a Local Church Consultation on Community Involvement

In many congregations, the initiative and work done on social concerns and community involvement will be carried out by a small group of members, a task force, or a committee. Not many are called and few are chosen for social action by the church.

This is just the way things are: Congregations normally structure their lives according to the many organizational maintenance functions required, and also according to church program elements deemed part of their reason for existing. Social concerns are only one element of the church's mission, albeit an important part of the whole body of Christ.

A social concerns group should function as an integral part of the whole body, and also on behalf of the entire congregation at times. In other words, you want to recognize your legitimate role as part of the mission of the church. *That means being accepted and supported by the congregation* rather than merely tolerated or, worse yet, being rejected and opposed as a suspect alien group doing things that are foreign to the nature of the church. Don't allow yourself to become alienated inside the church.

A social concerns group also needs to have limited freedom to act in the name of the whole congregation as specialists who represent the church in the community. *That means being trusted and authorized by the congregation* rather than merely being allowed or, worse yet, being disowned when you act for justice in the community and cause some controversy or bad publicity. Don't allow yourself to be cut off while out on a limb in the community.

Local Church Consultation

In order to achieve both acceptance and authorization by the congregation, and to lessen the twin dangers of either antagonism at home or betrayal while abroad, the social concerns group is well advised to court the heart of the congregation and to stimulate its mind. One of the ways to accomplish this is by means of a local church consultation on community involvement. It is essentially an educational task and event. Knowledge nurtures human interest and involvement begets loyalty, and you want to have both among the congregation.

Your pastor and some of your church members will have educational skills and experience to offer in the planning of such a consultation, so use them. This consultation will not be "a pat, precooked, minute-by-minute session plan to which you can just add water and serve." More helpful and freeing are some good suggestions of possible consultation components that you may want to include and shape according to your needs and style.

Consultation Purpose

It is important to be clear about the purpose of the consultation and then to make the design serve those ends. *Begin by writing a list of objectives that are as simple, limited, and specific as you can possibly make them.*

Remember, one consultation alone can neither be all nor do all that needs to be done in order to transform a local church into a socially concerned and active congregation. Think of the consultation as one strategic step in a one- or two-year plan, not as a panacea. Don't set yourself up for disappointment or failure through unrealistic objectives.

Here are examples of some possible objectives for a one-day consultation on church and community involvement:

1. To increase the understanding and support for social concerns work among five of the leaders and opinion-makers in the congregation.

2. To have twenty-five participants meet and hear from selected people in the community who have firsthand knowledge of the community and its problems (both church members and nonmembers).

3. To review a summary of the findings of your social concerns group after it has explored and analyzed the community (chapters 2 and 3).

4. To recognize the congregation's present involvements in the community, to stimulate imagination of new things it might be able and willing to do, and to identify people who could work on those new things.

5. To remember and celebrate your faith roots and the biblical mandates for the caring church to be involved in the life of the community.

6. To make at least one decision about the work of the social concerns group, and another one about the involvement of the church in the community.

Participants

Who and how many will participate in the consultation? The number will depend on particular local church factors like size of membership, interest, and so forth. The only suggestion made here is that the consultation be limited to between twenty and twenty-five people at the most. That will allow everyone a chance to speak and enable the leaders to run the meeting informally.

Who attends may well be more important than *how many* are there. You will need to decide between the alternatives of an open invitation to all members, or a carefully selected list of people invited personally to attend the consultation. Either way, recruitment efforts can be made to secure participation by people who may help the cause. People like the following can be considered:

1. Members already involved in the community in terms of residence, employment, voluntary service, membership in community organizations, and so forth.

2. Members in leadership positions in the church or with access to the arenas where decisions are made on church budget and program priorities.

3. Nonmembers who have a good knowledge of the community, its people, and its problems and can serve as resource persons and speakers.

4. Members who are characterized by one or more of the following:

● experience and skills that the social concerns group needs
● strong convictions about church/community involvement
● recent new membership
● openness to innovation, creativity, new ideas, and the willingness to take risks
● a generally positive view of life, the future, and other people
● more concern about evangelism and social action than church maintenance and survival
● a sense of humor and a sense of reality

Bible Study

The Bible is variously used, misused, and even abused at times in the churches and by this society. What we bring to the study of the texts determines in large part what we are able to draw from Scripture. To one degree or another, we are all "ideological captives" who bring the mindset, values, and assumptions of our American way of life to Scripture as baggage. Then we are comforted to find that the Bible is wise enough to support what we already believe about the nature and purpose of human life.

The Bible radically questions our present social order and passionately envisions revolutionary change for justice in "a new heaven and a new earth." Therefore, as Robert McAfee Brown puts it:

> We read what we can bear to read, we hear what is tolerable to hear, and we evade (or 'spiritualize') those parts which leave us uncomfortable, if not outraged.[1]

A period of Bible study, along with worship, can help open the participants to the transforming power of God's Word, to the new creation God has promised, and therefore to some new ideas and feelings about your community.

Listed below are some study passages that can have power in terms of the church's ministry of caring for the com-

munity. Other appropriate passages are listed elsewhere in the appendices.

You may want to divide the participants into groups of three, giving several passages to each group (the same passage can go to several groups). Give these triads the following directions and at least a half hour to work on the task.

1. Work with these passages by addressing three basic interpretive questions to each text (it's all right if you don't use all your passages because this is not a test to be taken):

   a. *The Analytical Question:* What did the original speaker intend for the original audience of the text? Who were the speaker and the audience?

   b. *The Imaginative Question:* How does this text continue to speak to us and throw light on life in our world today?

   c. *The Faith Question:* How does this text speak to our congregation about God's purpose and claim upon us? To what newness of life are we being called by this text?

2. Ask someone in your triad to report briefly your insights to the whole group after it reconvenes.

Suggested passages for biblical reflection:

Ecclesiastes 4:9-10	Lifting the fallen
Leviticus 19:33-34	Loving the foreigner
Ephesians 2:11-12	Identifying with foreigners
Colossians 3:11-12	Breaking down barriers
Matthew 25:31-45	Ministering to the needy
Luke 16:19-31	Helping the poor
Psalm 72:1-4	Championing the oppressed
Isaiah 1:15-17	Doing justice
Amos 8:4-10	Justice and judgment
Luke 4:16-21	The liberating gospel

Other Consultation Components

Here are some seedling ideas for options to help accomplish your particular objectives for the church and community consultation.

1. Give your pastor some brief air time to speak in support of new church initiatives in the community. Ask for a pep talk rather than a sermon or a lecture.

2. Plan a highly visual and summary way to brief the consultation on the findings of your social concerns group exploration of the community and its problems.

3. Think of what kinds of basic research data and findings on the community can be duplicated and distributed to the participants two weeks before the consultation as required reading.

4. Recruit some outside speakers and resource persons who have experiential knowledge of the community and its problems, who will speak with authority on both matters.

5. Present three people who have been affected by problems of the community. Give each person ten minutes to

tell his or her story. Invite them to stay for questions.

6. Put your "Power Map of the Community" up in a prominent place, explain what it says to you, and point out the locations of the people, powers, and principalities named during the consultation discussions.

7. Prepare a chart in pie shape showing the current budget components of your local church. Identify the size of "the pie piece" representing program monies expended on the local community people outside the church membership.

8. Prepare a "People Map of the Community" showing the present involvements of congregants in the community and what they are doing. Celebrate them!

9. Draw up a "Powerful Forces List." The purpose of this exercise is to have the participants discover and name *the five people, powers, or policies* that have the greatest potential for good or ill on the people and life of the community.

10. Wrap up the consultation with a Communion service. The bread and cup can remind us that in our faith, Jesus Christ is the last necessary victim of the powers of sin and death. In the bread and wine we are shown God's own possibilities and the promise of a new human community of love, peace, and justice for all.

Additional Resource

Owen D. Owens, "Five Steps to Becoming a Loving People," Literature Service Item LS22-304, $1.00, Judson Book Stores, P.O. Box 851, Valley Forge, PA 19481-0851

Appendix I
Action-Objectives

When you write your action-objectives, remember that verbs control objectives. The following five principles will help you to select verbs which will move you out into action.

When you write objectives:

1. Avoid verbs which point to an outcome beyond the ability of the planner to achieve. Some of these verbs are:

     request
     invite
     persuade
     offer

   RECOMMENDATION: Don't use these verbs.

2. Avoid verbs which describe a process but *not* the outcome for which the process is undertaken. Some of these verbs are:

     seek
     try to
     survey
     discuss
     review
     continue
     grow
     deepen
     advance
     serve
     encourage
     influence

   RECOMMENDATION: Press for the verb which gives the reason *why* behind the process verb. Example: "Try to recruit three persons . . ." becomes "Enlist three persons. . . ."

3. Avoid verbs which express results so vague that people cannot agree on what is meant.

     appreciate
     understand
     know

   RECOMMENDATION: Don't use these verbs.

4. Avoid verbs which are limited to thinking rather than acting.

     investigate
     study
     examine
     think about
     consider

   RECOMMENDATION: Save these verbs for first steps in your Program Plans.

5. Avoid verbs which express change *unless* you clearly state your starting point, the time period to be used, *and* the amount of change you want.

     increase
     deepen
     enhance
     preserve
     support
     maintain
     decrease
     reduce

   RECOMMENDATION: Be sure you specify your starting point, the time period needed, and the amount of change you want. Example: "Increase our visiting teams" becomes "Increase our visiting teams from two teams to four teams in six months."

Appendix J
Why Plans Fail*

Central to improving how you plan is finding out why some plans fail. It is simple enough: discover what contributes to failure and what must be done to reduce the possibility of failure. Failure is a certainty if you don't work hard, but simply working harder is not enough. Working smarter is essential. You can work smarter by learning from seven basic reasons why plans fail.

1. *No Real Goals* . . . therefore, no *real* plan. If there is no plan, the plan can't fail, but you can. Oddly enough many goal-setters don't actually know what a real goal is. They may point to some ideal mission such as "improve," "grow," or "increase ministry," but words this vague result in fantasies instead of goals. If your goal statement does not describe a condition or an end-state you want, it is *not* a goal.

2. *No Measurable Objectives.* If you don't know just what you intend to do, you will never know if you did it. Objectives are the guides to action. They must contain "action" verbs; without such action there will be little movement toward goal accomplishment. Objectives must be stated so they are measurable.

3. *Failure to Anticipate Obstacles.* No one can think of every contingency. Rash enthusiasm hampers a sensible effort to take account of possible obstacles and pitfalls. Every plan, no matter how carefully prepared, has limitations and built-in conflicts over priorities and resources. Planners who identify possible obstacles and ways to overcome them have superior batting averages. Effective planners take what at first they perceive to be large obstacles and break them down into small hurdles. They then develop ways to overcome each one. In short, a plan should be flexible enough to handle obstacles, whether anticipated or not.

4. *Lack of Milestones for Progress Reviews.* Plans that fail often have no concrete milestones or dates to review progress. Or milestones are allowed to slip by unnoticed. Famous last words in planning include: "It can wait," "I can remember that," or "I know how I'm doing." Periodic reviews of progress can alert you to the need for adjusting your plans or even your objectives. Milestones reached provide an important sense of accomplishment and desire to succeed further. Effective progress reviews provide a test of direction and pace. They also provide a check on the reality of the plan as you move along.

5. *Lack of Commitment.* Personal commitment is critical to the success of any plan. Laity may be hindered in long-range planning without a personal commitment from the pastor to support the process; the reverse is also true. Commitment means the willingness to see a plan through to completion. Commitment is stimulated by taking part in developing goals and objectives. Involve as many persons as possible in the goal and objective writing process.

6. *Failure to Revise Objectives.* A sure way to torpedo the best-laid plan is failure to restudy and reset objectives when indicated by new facts. Failure results when plans are not flexible enough to respond to changes in circumstances. It is important to rewrite objectives when necessary.

7. *Failure to Learn from Experience.* Failure to learn from experience arises when planners are unwilling to change their way of doing things. Many take comfort in the thought: "It's worked before; therefore it must be right." This attitude, however, will prevent you from ever finding out if "it is right" for this time until it is too late.

Summary

Learning how to plan is easy. Learning how to prevent plans from failing is difficult. The seven basic reasons why plans fail are shown in the chart. The symptoms which signal their presence and some of the best cures now available are also shown.

*Adapted from *New Venture Creation* by Jeffry A. Timmons; Leonard E. Smollen; and Alexander L. M. Dingee, Jr. (Homewood, Ill.: Richard D. Irwin, Inc., 1977), chapter 6; used with the authors' permission.

PLANNING: ITS REASONS FOR FAILURE, SYMPTOMS, AND CURES

REASONS FOR FAILURE	SYMPTOMS	CURES
1) No Real Goals	• Do not reflect the church's purpose statement • Talk about program plans • Are vague—sound good; say little • Completely beyond the reach of the church • Not "owned" by membership	• Relate goal to purpose statement • Rewrite goals so they describe end-states you want to reach or conditions you want to bring about • Involve more persons in goal writing
2) No Measurable Objectives	• Are not related to a goal • Are not measurable, specific, or time-phased • Do not contain action verbs	• Build each objective from a goal • Answer in objectives such questions as: Who? How many? Where? When? • Identify short term and long term objectives • Use action verbs in the statement
3) Failure to Anticipate Obstacles	• Excessive optimism • Closing your eyes to conflicts • Completion dates not met • "Ooops, I forgot!" • Didn't get support when needed • Crises are common	• Take time to list possible obstacles • Prepare ways to overcome listed obstacles • Be realistic in setting dates • Check Program Plan Details • Talk to Program Plan Manager • Revise Program Plan or Details
4) Lack of Milestones and Progress Reviews	• Completion dates not set • "It can wait;" "I can remember that" • "Let's play this by ear" • Don't really know how you are doing • Everything is short-term; no long-term aspects • Don't remember when the last review took place • No plans revised recently	• Set specific task milestones; stick to them • See that the Program Plan Manager is on the job • Review your progress on the dates set • Ask the question: Are we making enough progress toward the objective?

5) Lack of Commitment	• Putting things off • Just doing daily, routine activities • "I don't care what happens" • Have not set priorities • Planners skip meetings • No reports submitted • Pastor or lay members don't "own" the plan	• Involve others in the planning process • Share proposed plans early so new ideas can influence their development • Give the small groups of your church a chance to discuss proposed plans • Talk with each team member to find out the level of his/her commitment • Recruit replacements, as necessary • Celebrate successes you've had
6) Failure to Revise Objectives	• Plans never change • Being inflexible, refusing to face new facts that call for change • No sense of movement toward objectives • Help not sought when needed • Waste time on programs that don't work • Programs don't fit your priorities	• Deliberately seek feedback • Compare feedback with your standards for achieving the objective • Change emphasis and approach when it is appropriate • Encourage Program Plan Managers to alert Planning Task Force when revision is needed • Review progress more often
7) Failure to Learn from Experience	• Lose sight of goals • Repeat mistakes • Feedback is ignored • Evaluation standards are not used • Face the same crisis again and again • Unwillingness to change ways of doing things • Never asking, "What did we learn this time?"	• Use milestones to review progress • Have program units, task forces, etc., meet with the Planning Task Force • Keep a record of changes made as a result of evaluation • Concentrate on results, not on giving reports for their own sake

Appendix K
A Local Church Advocacy Policy

The local church advocacy model[1] outlined below shows some remarkable creativity and freedom on a matter that is difficult for many churches and taboo in some. The plan, developed by the session of Davis Community Church, a congregation of the Presbyterian Church (U.S.A.), shows a genuine concern for the involvement of the church and members in understanding and action on issues and problems of the community. It was based on a mission statement that included these words as one of its church and society objectives:

"To help persons think theologically about social and political issues in our society and to effect changes consistent with the Good News of God's love in Jesus Christ."

The advocacy policy they adopted to facilitate this objective encourages members to become informed about public issues and to form inquiry/action groups in the congregation, or in cooperation with other congregations. These groups are expected to stay alive by action on the issues. Neither the congregation nor the session endorses the specific positions and actions of these inquiry/action groups; they only emphasize that Christians should organize to study and act. Furthermore, the policy encourages members to join with people and organizations outside the church who seek to inform the churches and enlist their support for causes that are consonant with the church's work of reconciliation in society.

The advocacy policy is governed by the following guidelines:

1. Any two or more members of the congregation may organize on behalf of any cause, project, or candidate that they believe is furthering the will of God. Members must request the Church and Society Commission for recognition as an inquiry/action group, and be guided by these basic principles:

   a. Inquiry/action groups speak on behalf of their members only, and may not use the name of the congregation, the denomination, or the session. If requested, they shall provide the session with their membership list.

   b. Recognized inquiry/action groups are free to use the church bulletin boards, mailing lists, duplicating services, and church newsletter space within reasonable limits which will be determined by the session.

   c. Inquiry/action groups may relate to and include groups from other churches of this or other denominations, and also secular groups that share mutual concerns.

   d. The clergy and other church staff are free to work with any group by choice, and any group may receive minimal staff services upon request.

   e. If the session believes that an inquiry/action group is diametrically opposed to its understanding of the gospel as interpreted by the confessions of the church, the session has the right and the duty to declare its conscience on appropriate matters of doctrine and conduct.

2. This congregation is open to nonmembers and outside groups seeking support for their social action cause. However, the session must be requested and grant permission before such persons or groups may hold a meeting in the church, distribute information, or circulate a petition (unless the session has already taken action to endorse the cause involved).

3. The session desires to create an open climate where advocates of all sides of an issue are free to be represented. Events sponsored by a particular political party or promotion of a particular candidate for political office are prohibited. Bipartisan and nonpartisan discussions of candidates and the issues are permitted.

4. All activity protected by this policy shall be open to all interested persons and public notice shall be given for each meeting/event. Secret and closed activities are prohibited.

5. The session reserves the right to review and limit inquiry/action groups in terms of (a) the duration of the recognition granted by the Church and Society Commission, and (b) those actions that the session deems inappropriate.

The session of this local church also adopted a list of more specific rules governing the inquiry/action groups with regard to announcements, access to church budget monies and staff time, and use of church space. They cannot be reproduced here but may be obtained along with the original action of the session from the Program Agency, the Presbyterian Church (U.S.A.).

This model finds ways to nurture freedom within limits, to expect genuine newness within the historic confessional tradition, and to encourage Christian social action within the sphere and agenda of the secular world. Consider how you might use it as a starting point in formulating an advocacy policy for your local church.

Appendix L

Training and Fund-Raising Resources
for Community Organization

Training Assistance

The Interreligious Foundation for Community Organization (IFCO) is a national ecumenical organization devoted exclusively to providing technical assistance, management training, and fund-raising counsel for organizing poor and working-class people to make social changes. Established in 1966 as a nonprofit educational and charitable institution, IFCO has helped more than ten thousand organizations in all regions of the United States, Puerto Rico, and several foreign countries. Training programs are offered in proposal writing, church fund raising, foundation fund raising, and nonprofit accountancy and management. Information may be obtained from:

> IFCO
> 402 West 145th Street, 3rd Floor
> New York, NY 10031
> (212) 926-5757

Fund-Raising Resources

Pendleton, Niel, *Fund Raising: A Guide for Non-Profit Organizations* (Englewood Cliffs: Prentice-Hall, Inc., 1981) is a volume that is intended to help both the novice and the seasoned professional in the fund-raising process for either capital or annual funds. It provides an overview of campaigning and also includes a chapter on ''Looking to Foundations, Corporations, and Government'' which identifies other helpful resources for making and submitting proposals.

Appendix M
Suggested Resources

Bruland, Esther Byle, and Mott, Stephen Charles, *A Passion for Jesus; A Passion for Justice*. Valley Forge: Judson Press, 1983.

Fagan, Harry, *Empowerment: Skills for Parish Social Action*. Ramsey, N.J.: Paulist Press, 1979.

Hessel, Dieter T., ed., *Participants' Manual for Social Ministry Institutes*. New York: The Program Agency, The United Presbyterian Church, U.S.A.

Hessel, Dieter T., ed., *Rethinking Social Ministry*. New York: The Program Agency, The United Presbyterian Church, U.S.A. 1980.

Hessel, Dieter T., *A Social Action Primer*. Philadelphia: The Westminster Press, 1972.

Hessel, Dieter T., *Social Ministry*. Philadelphia: The Westminster Press, 1982.

Leas, Speed B., *Leadership and Conflict*. Nashville: Abingdon Press, 1982.

Light, Paul, ed., *Report of a 1981 Survey, New Church Development Research Project*, (Valley Forge: National Ministries, The American Baptist Churches, USA, 1982).

Macmanus, Shelia, *Community Action Sourcebook*. Ramsey, N.J.: Paulist Press, 1982.

McIntosh, Duncan, and Rusbuldt, Richard E., *Planning Growth in Your Church*. Valley Forge: Judson Press, 1983.

Nelson, Virgil and Lynn, *Catalog of Creative Ministries*. Valley Forge: Judson Press, 1983.

Peck, George and Hoffman, John S., eds., *The Laity in Ministry*. Valley Forge: Judson Press, 1984.

Pendleton, Niel, *Fundraising: A Guide for Non-Profit Organizations*. Englewood Cliffs: Prentice-Hall, Inc., 1981.

Pierce, Gregory, F., *Activism That Makes Sense: Congregations and Community Organization*. Ramsey, N.J.: Paulist Press, 1984.

Robinson, Peter S., ed., *Foundation Guide for Religious Grant Seekers*. Chico, Calif.: Scholars Press, 1979.

Ryan, William, *Blaming the Victim*. New York: Random House, Inc., 1976.

Sharp, Gene, *The Politics of Nonviolent Action*. Boston: Porter Sargent Publishers, Inc., 1974.

Warren, Rachelle B. and Donald I., *The Neighborhood Organizer's Handbook*. Notre Dame: University of Notre Dame Press, 1977.

Notes

Preface

[1]*Apologeticus* XXXIX.
[2]William R. Herzog II, *Two Half-Gospels or a Whole?* National Ministries, American Baptist Churches, U.S.A., 1979).

Chapter Two

[1]Walter Rauschenbusch, *Christianity and the Social Crisis* (New York: Macmillan Company, 1924), p. 9.
[2]See Appendix A for information on how to secure census data.

Chapter Three

[1]Adapted from Douglas E. Bartlett, "Guidelines for Choosing Issues" reprinted in the *Participant's Manual for Social Ministry Institutes,* ed. by Dieter T. Hessel (New York: Program Agency Board, Presbyterian Church, U.S.A.)

Chapter Four

[1]Adapted from Gabriel Fackre, *The Christian Story* (Grand Rapids: Wm. B. Eerdmans Publishing Co., 1978), p. 160.

Chapter Five

[1]Paul Light, ed., "Report of a 1981 Survey—New Church Development Project," (National Ministries, American Baptist Churches, U.S.A., November 1982).
[2]*Ibid.*, pp. 5-6.
[3]Adapted from George M. Wilson, "Justice-Oriented Congregations," in *Rethinking Social Ministry,* ed. Dieter T. Hessel (New York: Program Agency Board, Presbyterian Church, U.S.A., 1980).
[4]Ambrose Bierce, *The Devil's Dictionary* (Owings Mills, Md.: Stemmer House, 1978).

Chapter Six

[1]Adapted from Dieter T. Hessel, *Social Ministry* (Philadelphia: The Westminster Press, 1982), p. 156.
[2]Walter Rauschenbusch, *The Righteousness of the Kingdom,* ed. Max Stackhouse (Nashville: Abingdon Press, 1968), p. 189.

Chapter Seven

[1]*Redlining* refers to the practice of a financial institution to deny mortgage and other consumer financing to a particular area considered to be declining and a poor credit risk.

Chapter Eight

[1]Martin Luther King, Jr., *Letter From Birmingham City Jail,* (Philadelphia: American Friends Service Committee), pp. 8, 11.

Chapter Nine

[1]Quoted by Dieter T. Hessel in *Social Ministry* (Philadelphia: The Westminster Press, 1982), p. 42, from Kenneth Underwood, *The Church, the University and Social Policy,* Vol. I (Middletown, Conn.: Wesleyan University Press, 1969).
[2]Adapted from Gregory F. Pierce, *Activism That Makes Sense* (Ramsey, N.J.: Paulist Press, 1984), and Dieter T. Hessel, *A Social Action Primer* (Philadelphia: The Westminster Press, 1972).

[3] Quoted by Dieter T. Hessel in *A Social Action Primer* (Philadelphia: The Westminster Press, 1972), p. 99, from Saul D. Alinsky, *Rules for Radicals* (New York: Random House, Inc., 1971).

Chapter Ten

[1] Adapted from David Berlew, "Leadership and Organizational Excitement," *The California Management Review,* 2 (Winter 1974).

[2] Adapted from Speed B. Leas, *Leadership and Conflict* (Nashville: Abingdon Press, 1982).

[3] For example, see Duncan McIntosh and Richard E. Rusbuldt, *Planning Growth in Your Church* (Valley Forge: Judson Press, 1983).

Chapter Eleven

[1] Davidson, Hull, Elly and Nead, "Recent Research on Local Church Involvement," in *Rethinking Social Ministry,* ed. Dieter T. Hessel (New York: Program Agency Board, Presbyterian Church, U.S.A., 1980).

[2] Adapted from Speed B. Leas, *Leadership and Conflict* (Nashville: Abingdon Press, 1982); Gregory F. Pierce, *Activism That Makes Sense,* (Ramsey, N.J.: Paulist Press, 1984).

Appendix A

The information included in Appendix A is supplied by Superintendent of Documents, U.S. Government Printing Office, Washington, DC 20402.

Appendix B

Rusbuldt, R.E.; Gladden, R.K.; and Green, N.M., *Local Church Planning Manual* (Valley Forge: Judson Press, 1977), Appendix H.

Appendix D

Rusbuldt, Gladden, Green, *Local Church Planning Manual,* Appendix F.

Appendix E

Rusbuldt, Gladden, Green, *Local Church Planning Manual,* Appendix F.

Appendix G

[1] Adapted from Richard Broholm, *Identifying Gifts and Arenas,* (Newton Centre, Mass.: Center for the Ministry of the Laity, Andover Newton Theological School, n.d.).

[2] *Ibid.*

Appendix H

[1] Brown, Robert McAfee, *Theology in a New Key* (Philadelphia: The Westminster Press, 1978), p. 81.

Appendix I

Rusbuldt, Gladden, Green, *Local Church Planning Mannual,* Appendix J.

Appendix J

Rusbuldt, Gladden, Green, *Local Church Planning Mannual,* Appendix K.

Appendix K

[1] Adapted from a paper entitled "Davis Community Church Advocacy Policy," reprinted in the *Participants' Manual for Social Ministry Institutes,* ed. Dieter T. Hessel (New York: Program Agency Board, Presbyterian Church, U.S.A.).